# 用美国幼儿园课本

# AMERICAN SCHOOL TEXTBOOK 学英语

# Listening & Speaking Key

[美] 普特莱克
韩国逸创文化 著

中国纺织出版社

**图书在版编目（CIP）数据**

用美国幼儿园课本学英语. step 1 / （美）普特莱克，韩国逸创文化著. —北京：中国纺织出版社，2015.9

ISBN 978-7-5180-1727-0

Ⅰ.①用… Ⅱ. ①普… ②韩… Ⅲ. ①英语课-学前教育-教学参考资料 Ⅳ. ①G613.2

中国版本图书馆CIP数据核字（2015）第140929号

原文书名：미국교과서 읽는 리스닝 & 스피킹 Preschool 예비과정 1
原作者名：Michael A. Putlack, e-Creative Contents

著作权合同登记号：图字：01-2014-5047

---

**策划编辑：** 张向红 **责任编辑：** 张向红
**责任设计：** 林昕瑶 **责任印制：** 储志伟

---

中国纺织出版社出版发行
地　　址：北京市朝阳区百子湾东里A407号楼
邮政编码：100124
销售电话：010－67004422 传真：010－87155801
http: //www.c-textilep.com
E-mail: faxing@c-textilep.com
中国纺织出版社天猫旗舰店
官方微博http: //weibo.com/2119887771
北京通天印刷有限责任公司印刷　各地新华书店经销
2015年9月第1版第1次印刷
开　　本：787×1092　1 / 16　印张：7.25
字　　数：200千字　定价：29.80元

---

凡购本书，如有缺页、倒页、脱页，由本社图书营销中心调换

American School Textbook

# Listening & Speaking Key

## Preschool

## The Best Preparation for Building Basic Listening and Speaking Skills

The Listening & Speaking Key preschool series is designed to help children, especially preschoolers and kindergarteners, communicate in English. This series helps children develop their listening and speaking skills in a fun and easy way.

### Features

- Learning high-frequency words that appear most often in print
- A step-by-step learning process involving the learning of words, sentences, and then questions and answers
- Building basic communication skills and listening comprehension skills
- Exciting topics for preschoolers and kindergarteners that focus on using sight words
- Various activities, including reading, listening, speaking, and writing exercises
- Full-color photographs and illustrations

# Table of Contents

Components Workbook for Daily Review • Answers and Scripts

| Unit | Let's Listen | Let's Listen More | Let's Speak |
|---|---|---|---|
| Unit 1<br>What Is It? | **What is it?**<br>· It's a lion. | **Is it a snake?**<br>· **Yes, it is.** It's a snake.<br>· **No, it isn't.** It's an elephant. | **What is it?**<br>· It's a tiger. |
| Unit 2<br>Who Are You? | **Who are you?**<br>· Hi. I'm Jane. I'm a girl. | **Do you have long hair?**<br>· **Yes, I do.** I have long hair.<br>· **No, I don't.** I have short hair. | **What's your name?**<br>· My name is Mimi. |
| Unit 3<br>Who's He? | **Who's he?**<br>· He's my father.<br>**Who's she?**<br>· She's my mother. | **What does he have?**<br>· He has a dog.<br>**What does she have?**<br>· She has a rabbit. | **Who's he?**<br>· He's my brother.<br>**What does he have?**<br>· He has a dog. |
| Unit 4<br>What Are You Doing? | **What are you doing?**<br>· I'm walking. | **What is he doing?**<br>· He's eating pizza.<br>**What is she doing?**<br>· She's drinking milk. | **What are you doing?**<br>· I'm walking. |
| Unit 5<br>What Are They Doing? | **What are they?**<br>· They are kangaroos. | **What are they doing?**<br>· They are jumping. | **What are they doing?**<br>· They are running. |
| Unit 6<br>I Like to Run. | **Can you run?**<br>· **Yes, I can.** I can run fast.<br>· **No, I can't.** I can swim fast. | **Do you like to sing?**<br>· **Yes, I do.** I like to sing.<br>· **No, I don't.** I like to dance. | **What can you do?**<br>· I can run fast. I like to run. |
| Unit 7<br>She Likes to Run. | **What do you see?**<br>· I see a girl. She runs fast. | **Does he like to sing?**<br>· **Yes, he does.** He likes to sing.<br>· **No, he doesn't.** He likes to dance. | **What do you see?**<br>· I see a girl. She likes to dance. |
| Unit 8<br>Where Did You Go? | **Where did you go yesterday?**<br>· I went to school. | **What did you do yesterday?**<br>· I had a party. | **What did you do yesterday?**<br>· I went to school. |

Let's start!

# What Is It?

## Listen to the Words.

a. **Listen** and **say** the words.

lion

giraffe

monkey

zebra

b. **Listen again** and **check** the correct pictures.

1.

☑

2.

3.

☐

☐

4.

# Listen to the Sentences.

a. **Listen** and **say** the sentences.

It's a lion.

It's a giraffe.

It's a monkey.

It's a zebra.

b. **Listen again** and **number** the correct pictures.

1

## Listen and Speak. Practice the questions and answers.

03

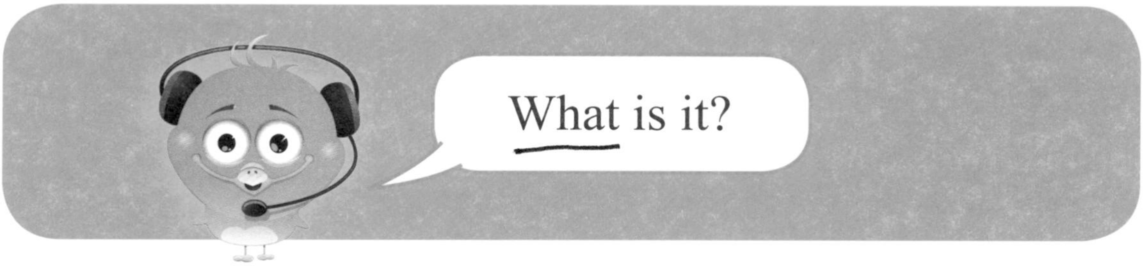

What is it?

1 It's **a lion**.

2 It's **a giraffe**.

3 It's **a monkey**.

4 It's **a zebra**.

# B Let's Listen More

## Listen to the Words.

04

a. **Listen** and **say** the words.

b. **Listen again** and **check** the correct pictures.

# Listen to the Sentences.

a. **Listen** and **say** the sentences.

It's a tiger.

It's an elephant.

It's a hippo.

It's a snake.

b. **Listen again** and **number** the correct pictures.

## Listen and Speak. Practice the questions and answers.

06

Is it a snake?
1 Yes, it is.
It's a snake.
2 No, it isn't.
It's an elephant.
Is it a hippo?
3 Yes, it is.
It's a hippo.
4 No, it isn't.
It's a tiger.

## C Listening Check-up

07

a. Listen and circle.

1.  a  b

2. a  b 

3. a  b 

b. Listen and answer. Then check.

1. 

- [x] Yes, it is.
- [ ] No, it isn't.

2. 

- [ ] Yes, it is.
- [x] No, it isn't.

Practice the questions and answers.

## Your Turn Ask and answer.

What is it?

# Who Are You?

## Listen to the Words.

a. **Listen** and **say** the words.

girl

boy

cat

dog

b. **Listen again** and **check** the correct pictures.

1.  ☑  ☐

2.   ☐  ☐

3.  ☐  ☐

4.  ☐  ☐

# Listen to the Sentences.

a. **Listen** and **say** the sentences.

I'm a girl.

I'm a boy.

I'm a cat.

I'm a dog.

b. **Listen again** and **number** the correct pictures.

## Listen and Speak. Practice the questions and answers.

Who are you?

1. Hi. I'm **Jane**.
   I'm **a girl**.

2. Hi. I'm **Tom**.
   I'm **a boy**.

3. Hi. I'm **Lulu**.
   I'm **a cat**.

4. Hi. I'm **Toto**.
   I'm **a dog**.

# B Let's Listen More

## Listen to the Words.

a. **Listen** and **say** the words.

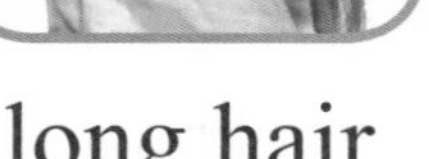

long hair | short hair | big eyes | big ears

b. **Listen again** and **check** the correct pictures.

1. 

2.   

3. 

4. 

# Listen to the Sentences.

13

a. **Listen** and **say** the sentences.

I have long hair.

I have short hair.

I have big eyes.

I have big ears.

b. **Listen again** and **number** the correct pictures.

## **Listen and Speak.** Practice the questions and answers.

14

**Do you** have long hair?

① **Yes, I do.**
I have long hair.

② **No, I don't.**
I have short hair.

**Do you** have big eyes?

③ **Yes, I do.**
I have big eyes.

④ **No, I don't.**
I have big ears.

## C Listening Check-up

15

a. Listen and circle.

b. **Find me.** Listen and number.

Practice the questions and answers.

Hi. I'm **Toto**.
What's your name?
My name is **Mimi**.


## Your Turn Ask and answer.

# Who's He?

## A Let's Listen

### Listen to the Words.

a. **Listen** and **say** the words.

b. **Listen again** and **check** the correct pictures.

1.  

2.  

3. 

4.  

# Listen to the Sentences.

a. **Listen** and **say** the sentences.

He's my father.

She's my mother.

He's my brother.

She's my sister.

b. **Listen again** and **number** the correct pictures.

1

## Listen and Speak. Practice the questions and answers.

19

Who's **he**?
1 **He**'s my father.
2 **He**'s my brother.
me
Who's **she**?
3 **She**'s my mother.
4 **She**'s my sister.
me

# B Let's Listen More

## Listen to the Words.

20

a. **Listen** and **say** the words.

b. **Listen again** and **check** the correct pictures.

# Listen to the Sentences.

21

a. **Listen** and **say** the sentences.

**My father** has a bird.
**He** has a bird.

**My mother** has a rabbit.
**She** has a rabbit.

**My brother** has a dog.
**He** has a dog.

**My sister** has a cat.
**She** has a cat.

b. **Listen again** and **number** the correct pictures.

## **Listen and Speak.** Practice the questions and answers.

What **does he have**?

① **He has** a dog.

② **He has** a cat.

What **does she have**?

③ **She has** a rabbit.

④ **She has** a bird.

## C Listening Check-up

23

a. Listen and circle.

1.  

b 

2. a 

b 

3. a 

b 

b. Listen and check the correct pictures.

1.  

2.  

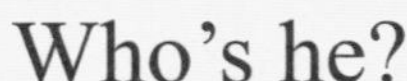


## D Let's Speak

Practice the questions and answers. 24

Who's he?

He's my brother.

What does he have?

He has a dog.

## Your Turn

Ask and answer.

Who's she?
________

me

Who's he?
________

What does she have?
________

What does he have?
________

# What Are You Doing?

## Listen to the Words.

a. **Listen** and **say** the words.

walking running singing dancing

b. **Listen again** and **check** the correct pictures.

1.    

2.   

3.  

4.  

# Listen to the Sentences.

26

a. **Listen** and **say** the sentences.

I'm walking.

I'm running.

I'm singing.

I'm dancing.

b. **Listen again** and **number** the correct pictures.

1

## Listen and Speak. Practice the questions and answers.

27

What are you **doing**?

1 I'm **walking**.

2 I'm **running**.

3 I'm **singing**.

4 I'm **dancing**.

## B Let's Listen More

# Listen to the Words.

a. **Listen** and **say** the words.

eating

drinking

cooking

washing

b. **Listen again** and **check** the correct pictures.

1.

2.

3.

4.

# Listen to the Sentences.

a. **Listen** and **say** the sentences.

He's **eating pizza**.

She's **drinking milk**.

He's **cooking**.

She's **washing the dishes**.

b. **Listen again** and **number** the correct pictures.

1

## Listen and Speak. Practice the questions and answers.

What is he **doing**?

1 He's **eating ice cream**.

2 He's **drinking water**.

What is she **doing**?

3 She's **cooking**.

4 She's **washing the dishes**.

## C Listening Check-up

31

a. Listen and circle.

1. a

b

2. a

b

3. a

b

b. Listen and check the correct pictures.

1.

☑ ☐

2.

☐ ☐

Practice the questions and answers.

## Your Turn

Ask and answer.

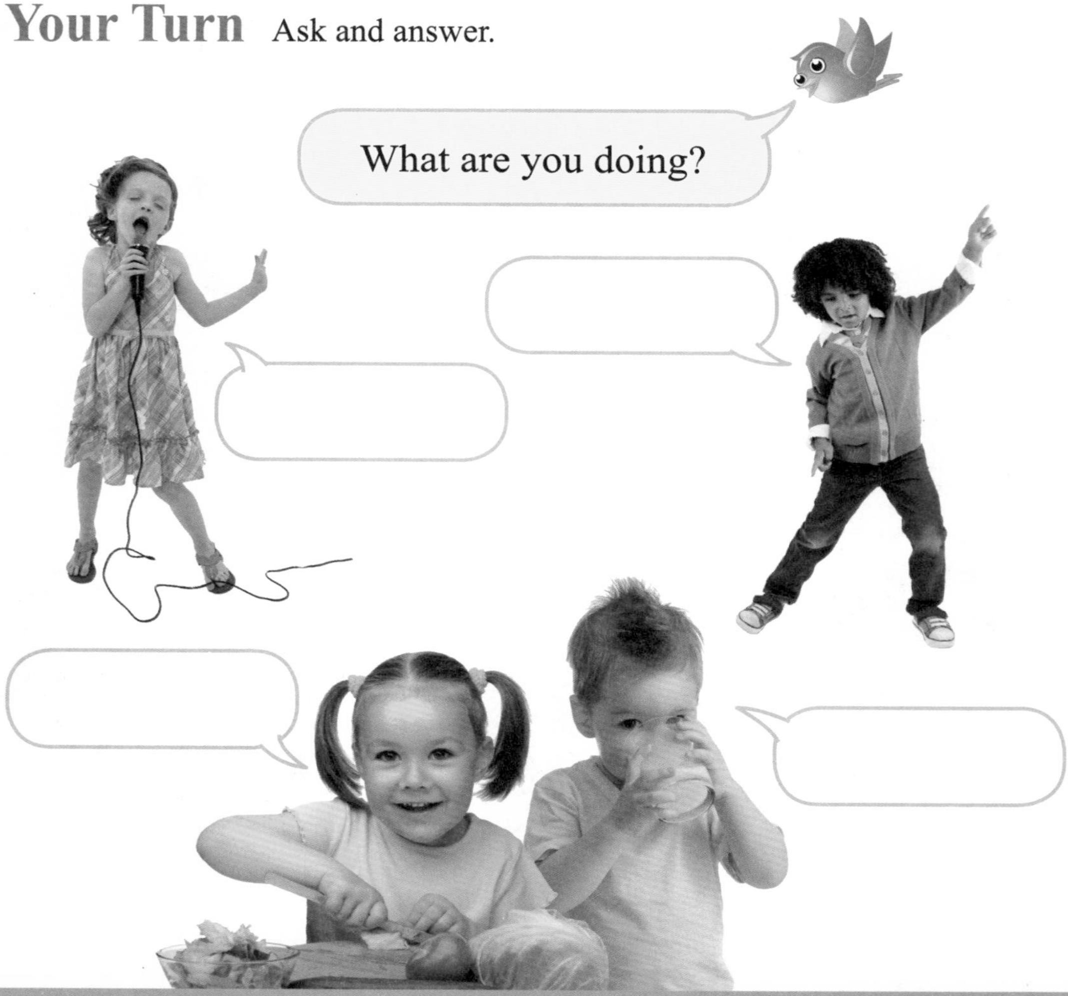

What are you doing?

# What Are They Doing?

## Listen to the Words.

a. **Listen** and **say** the words.

kangaroos

birds

koalas

dolphins

b. **Listen again** and **check** the correct pictures.

1. 

2. 

3. 

4. 

# Listen to the Sentences.

a. **Listen** and **say** the sentences.

They are kangaroos.

They are birds.

They are koalas.

They are dolphins.

b. **Listen again** and **number** the correct pictures.

1

## Listen and Speak. Practice the questions and answers.

35

What are they?
① They are **kangaroos**.
② They are **koalas**.
③ They are **birds**.
④ They are **dolphins**.

## B Let's Listen More

# Listen to the Words.

a. **Listen** and **say** the words.

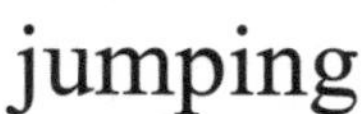
jumping

flying

sleeping

swimming

b. **Listen again** and **check** the correct pictures.

1.
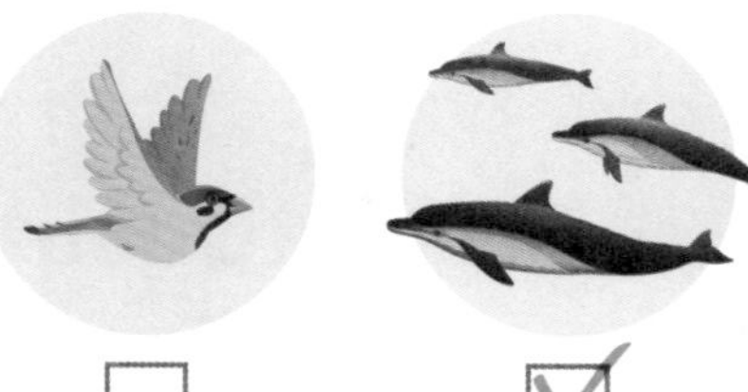

2.
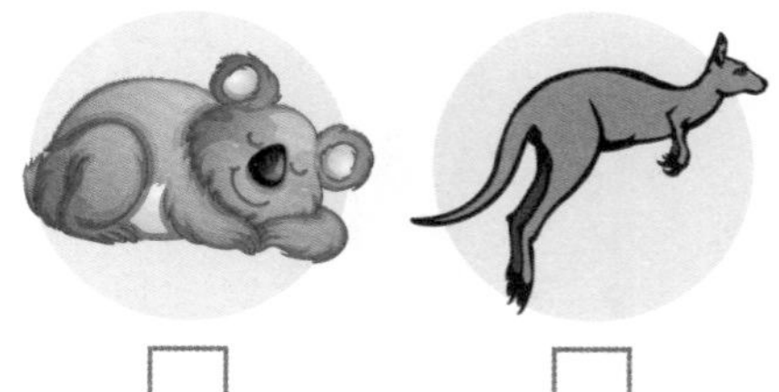

3.

4.

# Listen to the Sentences.

a. **Listen** and **say** the sentences.

**The kangaroos** are jumping.
**They** are jumping.

**The birds** are flying.
**They** are flying.

**The koalas** are sleeping.
**They** are sleeping.

**The dolphins** are swimming.
**They** are swimming.

b. **Listen again** and **number** the correct pictures.

## Listen and Speak. Practice the questions and answers.

38

What are they **doing**?

① They are **jumping**.

② They are **swimming**.

③ They are **flying**.

④ They are **sleeping**.

## C Listening Check-up

39

a. Listen and circle.

1. a  b 

2. a  b 

3. a  b 

b. Listen and check the correct pictures.

1. 

2.  

Practice the questions and answers.

## Your Turn

Ask and answer.

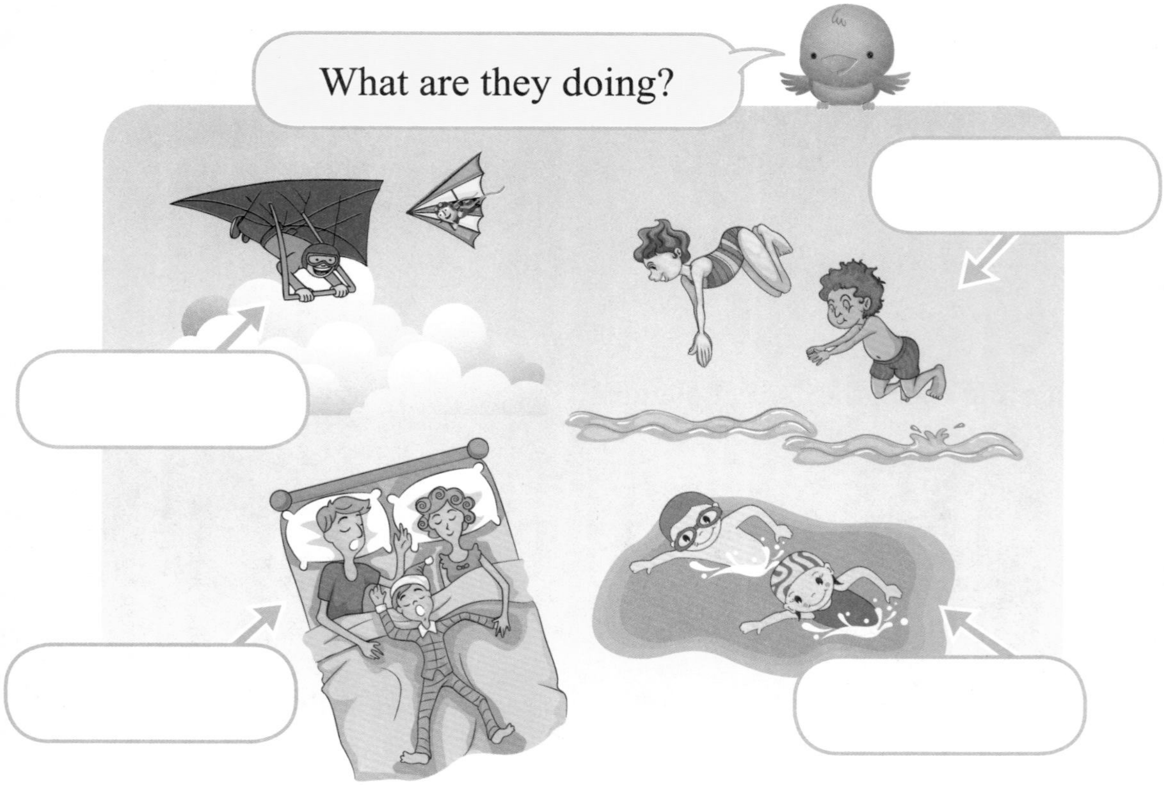

What are they doing?

# I Like to Run.

## Listen to the Words.

a. **Listen** and **say** the words.

run

fly

jump

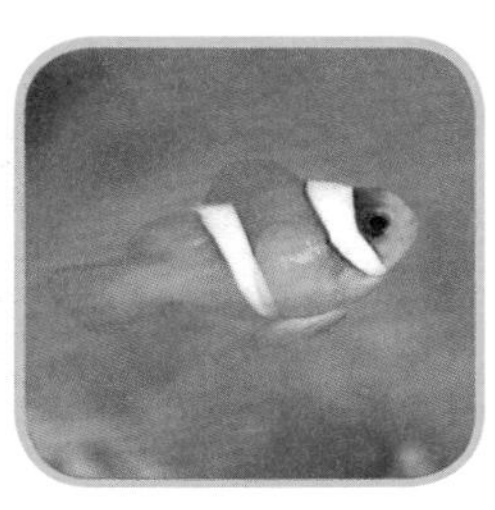

swim

b. **Listen again** and **check** the correct pictures.

1.

☐ ☑

2.

☐ ☐

3.

☐ ☐

4.

☐ ☐

# Listen to the Sentences.

a. **Listen** and **say** the sentences.

I can run.

I can fly.

I can jump.

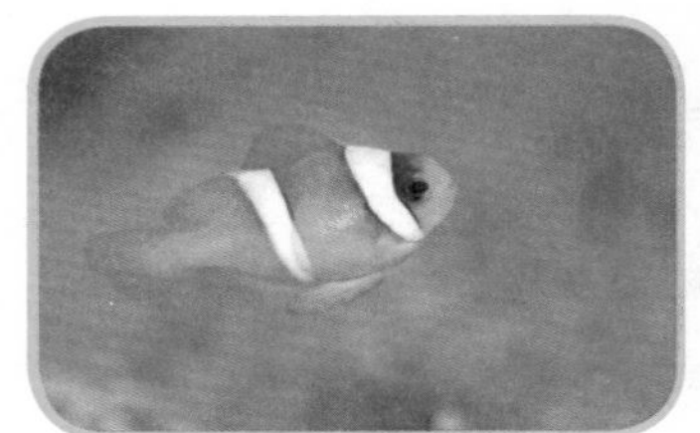

I can swim.

b. **Listen again** and **number** the correct pictures.

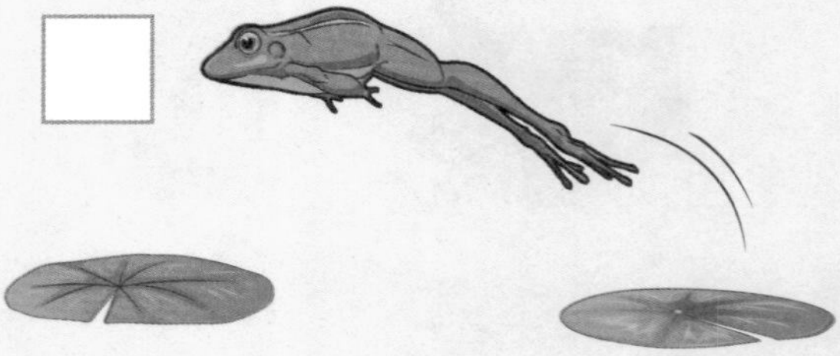

1

## Listen and Speak. Practice the questions and answers.

**Can you** run?

1 **Yes, I can.**
I can run fast.

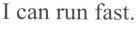

2 **No, I can't.**
I can swim fast.

**Can you** fly?

3 **Yes, I can.**
I can fly high.

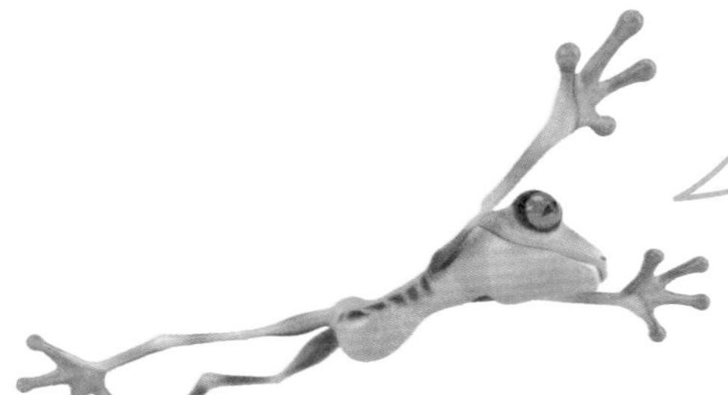

4 **No, I can't.**
I can jump high.

# B Let's Listen More

## Listen to the Words.

a. **Listen** and **say** the words.

sing dance eat cook

b. **Listen again** and **check** the correct pictures.

# Listen to the Sentences.

45

a. **Listen** and **say** the sentences.

I **sing** well.
I **like to** sing.

I **dance** well.
I **like to** dance.

I **eat** well.
I **like to** eat.

I **cook** well.
I **like to** cook.

b. **Listen again** and **number** the correct pictures.

## **Listen and Speak.** Practice the questions and answers.

46

**Do you** like to sing?

1 **Yes, I do.**
I like to sing.

2 **No, I don't.**
I like to dance.

**Do you** like to cook?

3 **Yes, I do.**
I like to cook.

4 **No, I don't.**
I like to eat.

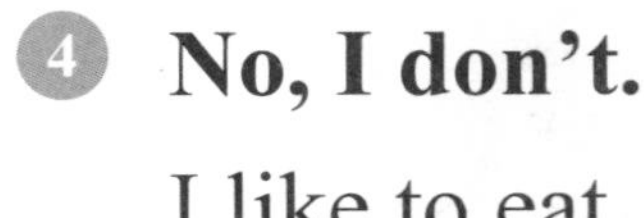

## C Listening Check-up

47

a. Listen and circle.

1. (a) 

b 

2. a 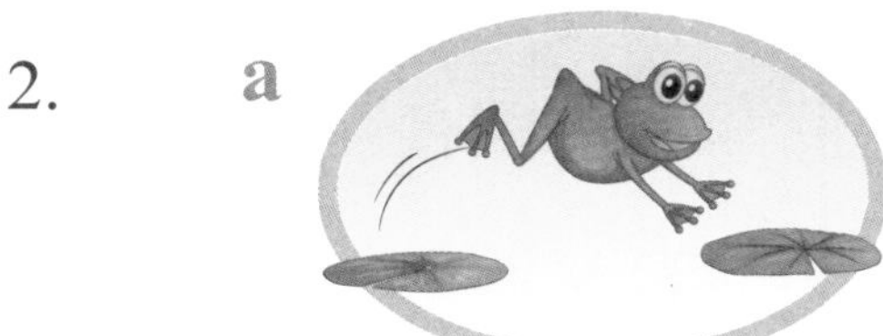

b 

3. a 

b 

b. Listen and check the correct pictures.

1. 

☑ ☐

2.  

☐ ☐

Practice the questions and answers.

What can you do?

**I can** run fast.
**I like to** run.

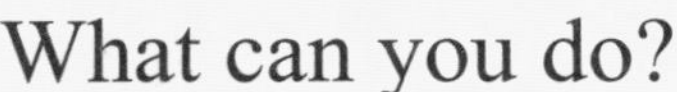

## Your Turn

Ask and answer.

What can you do?

# She Likes to Run.

## Listen to the Words.

a. **Listen** and **say** the words.

walks

runs

jumps

swims

b. **Listen again** and **check** the correct pictures.

1.

☑

☐

2.

☐ ☐

3.

☐

☐

4.

☐

☐

# Listen to the Sentences.

50

a. **Listen** and **say** the sentences.

The boy **walks**.
He **walks**.

The girl **runs**.
She **runs**.

The horse **jumps**.
It **jumps**.

The fish **swims**.
It **swims**.

b. **Listen again** and **number** the correct pictures.

## Listen and Speak. Practice the questions and answers.

What do you see?

1. I see **a boy**. **He walks** fast.

2. I see **a girl**. **She runs** fast.

3. I see **a horse**. **It jumps** well.

4. I see **a fish**. **It swims** well.

## B Let's Listen More

## Listen to the Words.

a. **Listen** and **say** the words.

sings

dances

eats

cooks

b. **Listen again** and **check** the correct pictures.

1.

2.

3.

4.

# Listen to the Sentences.

53

a. **Listen** and **say** the sentences.

He **sings** well.
He **likes to** sing.

She **dances** well.
She **likes to** dance.

He **eats** well.
He **likes to** eat.

She **cooks** well.
She **likes to** cook.

b. **Listen again** and **number** the correct pictures.

## Listen and Speak. Practice the questions and answers.

**Does he** like to sing?

① **Yes, he does.**
He likes to sing.

② **No, he doesn't.**
He likes to dance.

**Does she** like to cook?

③ **Yes, she does.**
She likes to cook.

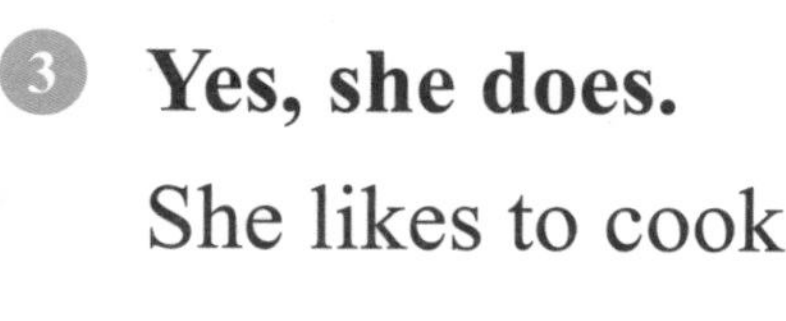

④ **No, she doesn't.**
She likes to eat.

## C Listening Check-up

55

a. Listen and circle.

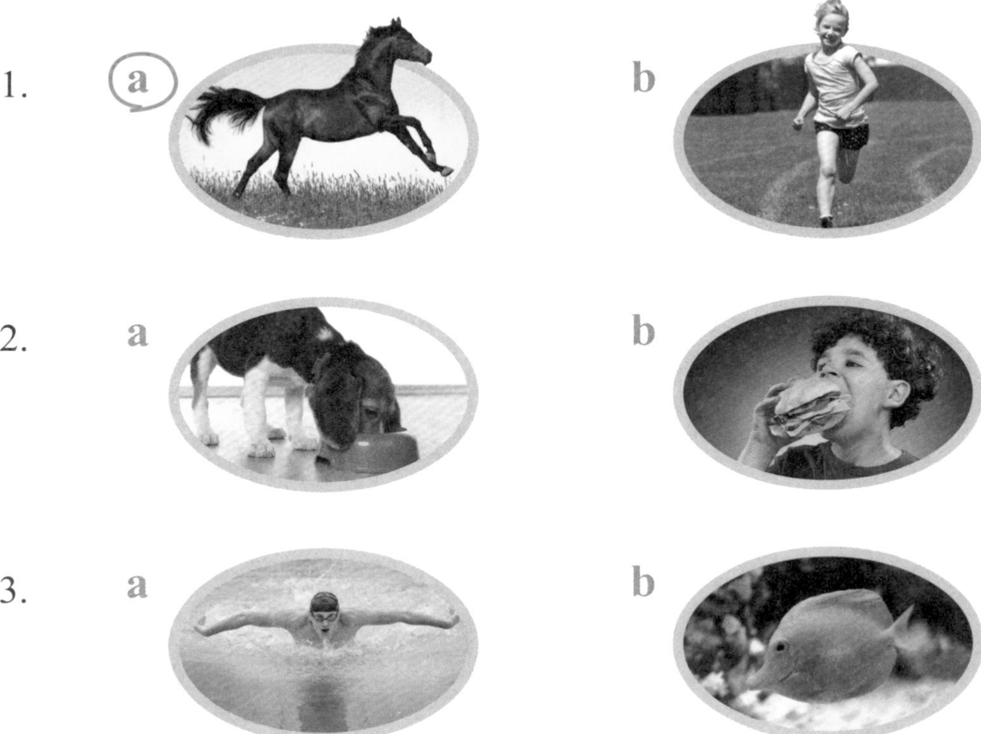


b. **What do you see?** Listen and number.

Practice the questions and answers.

What do you see?
I see **a girl**.
**She likes to** dance.


## Your Turn

Ask and answer.

What do you see?

# Unit 8 Where Did You Go?

## A Let's Listen

### Listen to the Words.

57

a. **Listen** and **say** the words.

go to school

go to the park

go to a movie

go to a party

b. **Listen again** and **check** the correct pictures.

1.

 ☐

 ☑

2.

 ☐

 ☐

3.

 ☐

 ☐

4.

 ☐

 ☐

# Listen to the Sentences.

a. **Listen** and **say** the sentences.

| | Today | | Yesterday |
|---|---|---|---|
|  | I **go** to school. | ⇨ | I **went** to school. |
|  | I **go** to the park. | ⇨ | I **went** to the park. |
|  | I **go** to a movie. | ⇨ | I **went** to a movie. |
|  | I **go** to a party. | ⇨ | I **went** to a party. |

b. **Listen again** and **number** the correct pictures.

☐ 

 1

☐

☐

## Listen and Speak. Practice the questions and answers.

**Where did you go** yesterday?

① **I went** to school.

② **I went** to the park.

③ **I went** to a party.

④ **I went** to a movie.

# B Let's Listen More

## Listen to the Words.

a. **Listen** and **say** the words.

have a party

eat cake

play with friends

watch TV

b. **Listen again** and **check** the correct pictures.

1.

2.

3.

4.

# Listen to the Sentences.

a. **Listen** and **say** the sentences.

| | Today | | Yesterday |
|---|---|---|---|
|  | I **have** a party. | ⇨ | I **had** a party. |
|  | I **eat** cake. | ⇨ | I **ate** cake. |
|  | I **play** with my friends. | ⇨ | I **played** with my friends. |
|  | I **watch** TV. | ⇨ | I **watched** TV. |

b. **Listen again** and **number** the correct pictures.

## **Listen and Speak.** Practice the questions and answers.

**What did you do** yesterday?

① **I had** a birthday party.

② **I ate** cake.

③ **I played** with my friends.

④ **I watched** TV with my friends.

# C Listening Check-up

a. Listen and circle.

1. a 

b 

2. a 

b 

3. a 

b 

b. Listen and number.

## D Let's Speak Practice the questions and answers. 64

## Your Turn Ask and answer.

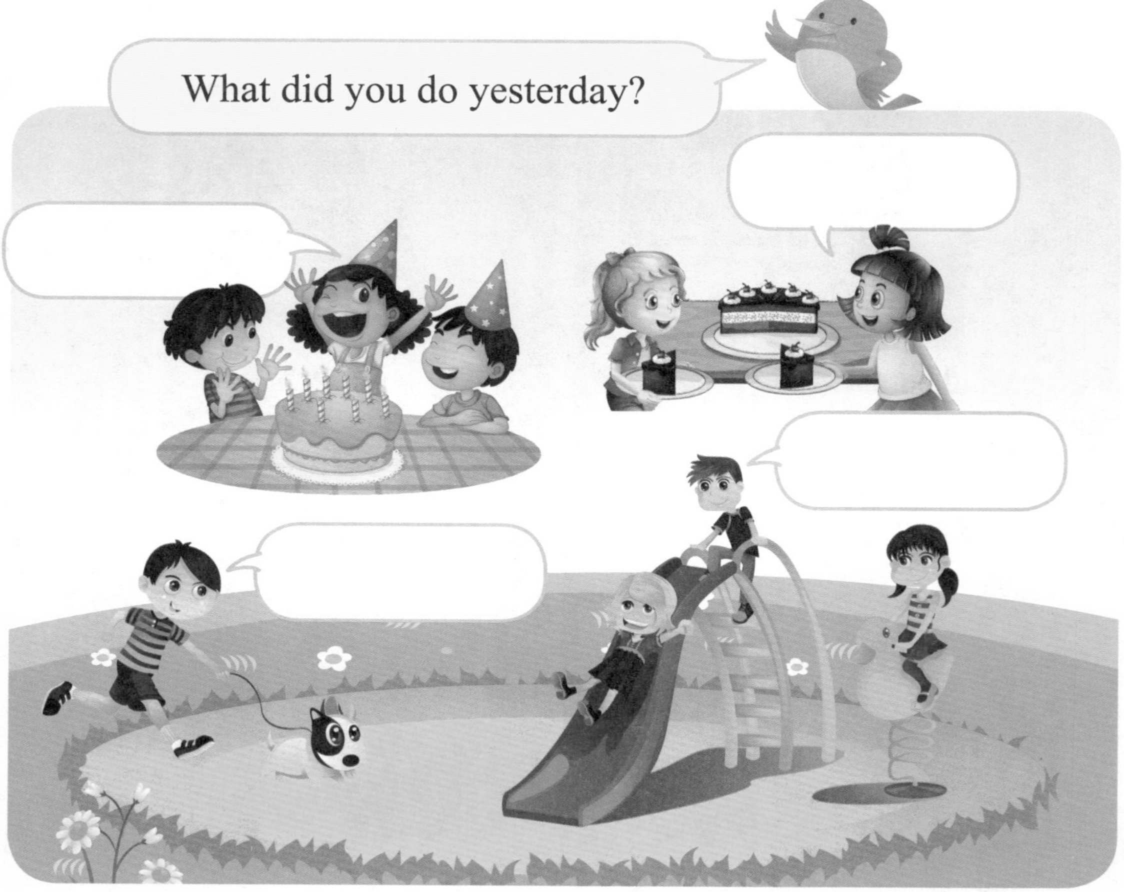

What did you do yesterday?

Word
List

Unit 1

## What Is It?

它是什么?

| | |
|---|---|
| **it** | 它 |
| **What is it?** | 它是什么? |
| **lion** | 狮子 |
| **giraffe** | 长颈鹿 |
| **monkey** | 猴子 |
| **zebra** | 斑马 |
| **It's ~ = It is ~** | 它是…… |
| **It's a lion.** | 它是一头狮子。 |
| **tiger** | 老虎 |
| **elephant** | 大象 |
| **hippo** | 河马 |
| **snake** | 蛇 |
| **Is it ~?** | 它是……吗? |
| **Is it a snake?** | 它是一条蛇吗? |
| **Yes, it is.** | 是的，它是。 |
| **No, it isn't.** | 不，它不是。 |

Unit 2

## Who Are You?

你是谁?

| | |
|---|---|
| **girl** | 女孩 |
| **boy** | 男孩 |
| **cat** | 猫 |
| **dog** | 狗 |
| **I'm ~ = I am ~** | 我是…… |
| **I'm a girl.** | 我是女孩。 |
| **I'm a boy.** | 我是男孩。 |
| **Hi.** | 嗨。 |
| **I'm Jane.** | 我是简。 |
| **long hair** | 长发 |
| **short hair** | 短发 |
| **big eyes** | 大眼睛 |
| **big ears** | 大耳朵 |
| **I have ~** | 我有…… |
| **I have long hair.** | 我有长发。 |
| **I have big eyes.** | 我有大眼睛。 |
| **Do you ~?** | 你……吗? |
| **Do you have long hair?** | 你有长发吗? |
| **Yes, I do.** | 是的，我有。 |
| **No, I don't.** | 不，我没有。 |
| **What's your name?** | 你的名字是什么? |
| **My name is Mimi.** | 我的名字是咪咪。 |

Unit 3

## Who's He?

他是谁?

**Who's ~? = Who is ~?** ……是谁?

**Who's he?** 他是谁?

**Who's she?** 她是谁?

**father** 父亲

**mother** 母亲

**brother** 兄弟

**sister** 姐妹

**me** 我

**He's ~ = He is ~** 他是……

**He's my father.** 他是我爸爸。

**She's ~ = She is ~** 她是……

**She's my mother.** 她是我妈妈。

**bird** 鸟

**rabbit** 兔子

**he** 他

**she** 她

**has** 有（单数第三人称）
* have有（原形）

**My father has a bird.** 我父亲有一只鸟。

**What does he have?** 他有什么?

**He has a dog.** 他有一只狗。

**What does she have?** 她有什么?

**She has a rabbit.** 她有一只兔子。

Unit 4

## What Are You Doing?

你在做什么?

**do** 做

**What are you doing?** 你在做什么?
***be** + 动词-**ing**: 正在……

**walking** 走
*walk走（动词原形）

**running** 跑
*run跑（动词原形）

**singing** 唱歌
*sing唱歌（动词原形）

**dancing** 跳舞
*dance跳舞（动词原形）

**I'm walking.** 我在走。

**eating** 吃
*eat吃（动词原形）

**drinking** 喝
*drink喝（动词原形）

**cooking** 做饭
*cook做饭（动词原形）

**washing** 洗
*wash洗（动词原形）

**He's -ing = He is -ing** 他正在……

**eat pizza** 吃比萨

**He's eating pizza.** 他在吃比萨。

**She's -ing = She is -ing** 她正在……

**drink milk** 喝牛奶

**She's drinking milk.** 她在喝牛奶。

wash the dishes 洗盘子（洗碗）

She's washing the dishes. 她在刷碗。

What is he doing? 他在干什么?

What is she doing? 她在干什么?

eat ice cream 吃冰淇淋

drink water 喝水

## What Are They Doing?

他们在干什么?

kangaroos 袋鼠

birds 鸟

koalas 考拉

dolphins 海豚 *dolphin的复数形式

They are ~ 他们是……

They are kangaroos. 他们是袋鼠。

What are they? 他们是什么?

jumping 跳
*jump跳（动词原形）

flying 飞
*fly飞（动词原形）

sleeping 睡觉
*sleep睡觉（动词原形）

swimming 游泳
*swim游泳（动词原形）

What are they doing? 他们在做什么?

Unit 6

## I Like to Run.

我喜欢跑步。

I like to ~ 我喜欢……

run 跑步

I like to run. 我喜欢跑步。

fly 飞

jump 跳

swim 游泳

I can ~ 我能……

I can run. 我能跑步。

Can you ~? 你能……吗?

Can you run? 你能跑步吗?

Yes, I can. 是的，我能跑。

No, I can't. 不，我不能跑。

run fast 跑得快

swim fast 游得快

fly high 飞得高

jump high 跳得高

sing 唱歌

dance 跳舞

eat 吃

cook 做饭

sing well 唱得好

dance well 跳得好

eat well 吃得好

cook well 做饭做得好

**I like to sing.** 我喜欢唱歌。

**Do you like to ~?** 你喜欢……吗?

**Do you like to sing?** 你喜欢唱歌吗?

**Yes, I do.** 是的，我喜欢。

**No, I don't.** 不，我不喜欢。

**What can you do?** 你能做什么?

## She Likes to Run.
她喜欢跑步。

**She likes to ~** 她喜欢……

**She likes to run.** 她喜欢跑步。

**walks** 走路 *walk第三人称单数

**runs** 跑步 *run第三人称单数

**jumps** 跳 *jump第三人称单数

**swims** 游泳 *swim第三人称单数

**The boy walks.** 男孩走路。

**He walks.** 他走着。

**horse** 马

**The horse jumps.** 马跳着。

**It jumps.** 它跳着。

**fish** 鱼 *复数: fish

**What do you see?** 你看到什么?

**I see ~** 我看到……

**sings** 唱歌 *sing第三人称单数

**dances** 跳舞 *dance第三人称单数

**eats** 吃 *eat第三人称单数

**cooks** 做饭 *cook第三人称单数

**He sings well.** 他唱得很好。

**He likes to sing.** 他喜欢唱歌。

**does** 做 *do第三人称单数

**Does he like to ~?**
他喜欢……吗?

**Does she like to ~?**
她喜欢……吗?

**Does he like to sing?**
他喜欢唱歌吗?

**Yes, he does.** 是的，他喜欢。

**No, he doesn't.** 不，他不喜欢。

## Where Did You Go?
你去哪里了?

**did** 做 *do过去时

**go** 去

**went** 去 *go过去时

**go to school** 去上学

**went to school** 去上学

**go to the park** 去公园

**went to the park** 去公园

**go to a movie** 去看电影

**went to a movie** 去看电影

**go to a party** 去派对

**went to a party** 去派对

**today** 今天

**yesterday** 昨天

**have** 助动词

**had** 助动词
*have过去时

**have a party** 举办派对

**had a party** 举办了一个派对

**eat** 吃

**ate** 吃 *eat过去时

**eat cake** 吃蛋糕

**ate cake** 吃蛋糕

**play** 玩

**played** 玩 *play过去时

**play with friends** 和朋友一起玩

**played with friends** 和朋友一起玩

**watch** 看

**watched** 看
*watch过去时

**watch TV** 看电视

**watched TV** 看电视

**What did you do yesterday?**
你昨天干什么了?

★ 为幼儿园小朋友准备的分阶段英语学习资料

# 用美国幼儿园课本学英语

AMERICAN SCHOOL TEXTBOOK

# Listening & Speaking Key

Preschool 学前班篇 1

## Workbook | 答案与译文

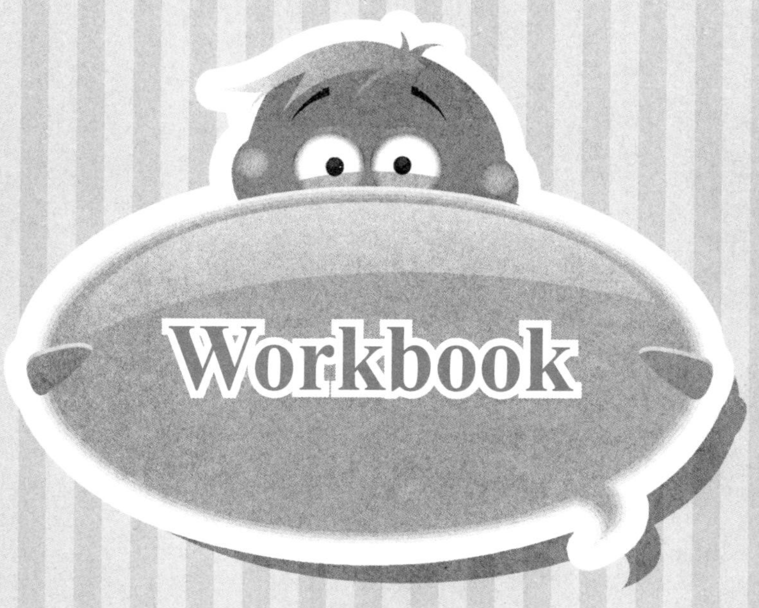
Workbook

Daily Test 1

# What Is It?

## A Listen, write, and match.

65

1. lion
2. ________
3. ________
4. ________
5. ________
6. ________
7. ________
8. ________

| lion | giraffe | monkey | zebra |
|---|---|---|---|
| tiger | elephant | hippo | snake |

## B Ask and answer the questions.

1. 

A: What is it?

B: It's a ________.

2. 

A: Is it an elephant?

B: Yes, ________. It's an elephant.

C Listen and circle the correct pictures. 66

1. Q: What is it?

a 

b 

c 

2. Q: What is it?

a 

b 

c 

D Listen and answer. Then check. 67

1. 

☐ Yes, it is.

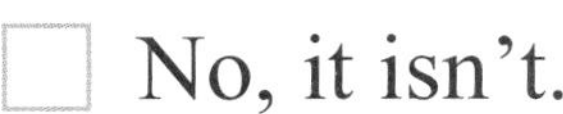

☐ No, it isn't.

2. 

☐ Yes, it is.

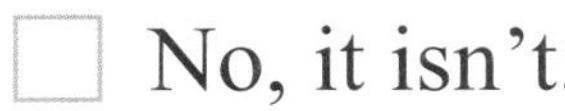

☐ No, it isn't.

3. 

☐ Yes, it is.

☐ No, it isn't.

Daily Test 2

# Who Are You?

## A Listen, write, and match.

68

1. girl
2. ________________
3. ________________
4. ________________
5. ________________
6. ________________
7. ________________
8. ________________

| girl | boy | short hair | long hair |
|---|---|---|---|
| cat | dog | big eyes | big ears |

## B Ask and answer the questions.

1. 

A: Who are you?

B: I'm ________ (your name). I'm a ________ (boy / girl).

2. 

A: What's your name?

B: My name is ________ (your name).

## C Listen and answer. Then check. 69

1. 

☐ Yes, I do.

☐ No, I don't.

2. 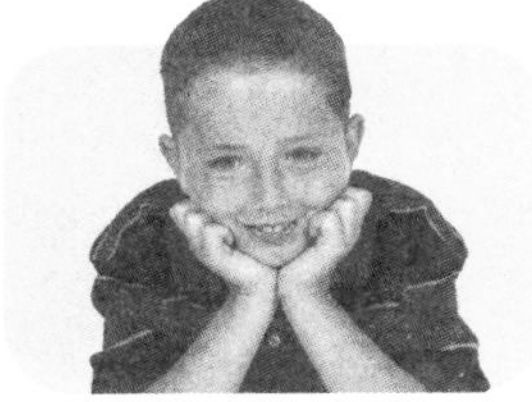

☐ Yes, I do.

☐ No, I don't.

3. 

☐ Yes, I do.

☐ No, I don't.

## D Listen and check the correct pictures. 70

1.  ☐ ☐

2.   ☐ ☐

3.  ☐ ☐

4.   ☐ ☐

# Daily Test 3 Who's He?

**A** Listen, write, and match. 71

1. my mother
2. ____________
3. ____________
4. ____________
5. ____________
6. ____________

| my father | my mother | bird |
|---|---|---|
| my brother | my sister | rabbit |

**B** Ask and answer the questions.

1. 

A: Who's he?

B: He's ____________.

A: What does he have?

B: He has ____________.

2. 

A: Who's she?

B: She's ____________.

A: What does she have?

B: She has ____________.

 Listen and circle the correct pictures. 72

1. Q: What does he have?

a  b  c 

2. Q: What does she have?

a  b  c 

D Listen and number the correct pictures. 73

# What Are You Doing?

## A Listen, write, and match.

74

1. walking
2. ______
3. ______
4. ______
5. ______
6. ______
7. ______
8. ______

| walking | running | singing | dancing |
| --- | --- | --- | --- |
| cooking | washing | eating | drinking |

## B Ask and answer the questions.

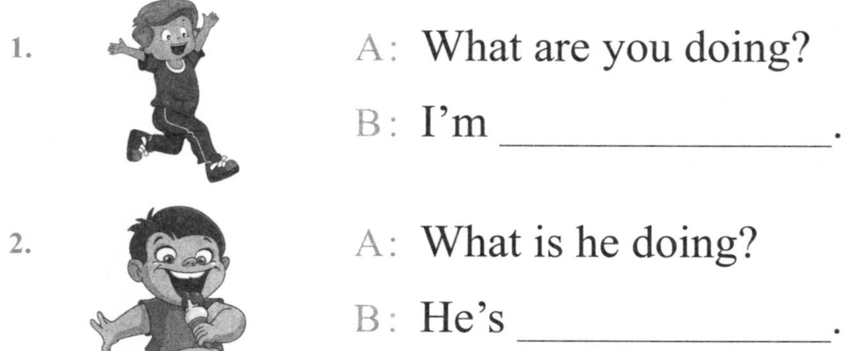

1. A: What are you doing?
   B: I'm ______.

2. A: What is he doing?
   B: He's ______.

C Listen and circle the correct pictures.

1. Q: What is she doing?

a 

b 

c 

2. Q: What is he doing?

a 

b 

c 

D Listen and check the correct pictures.

76

1.

2.

3.

4.

Daily Test 5

# What Are They Doing?

## A Listen, write, and match.

77

1. birds
2. ____________
3. ____________
4. ____________
5. ____________
6. ____________
7. ____________
8. ____________

| kangaroos | birds | koalas | dolphins |
| --- | --- | --- | --- |
| jumping | flying | swimming | sleeping |

## B Ask and answer the questions.

1. A: What are they?
   B: They are ____________.
2. A: What are they doing?
   B: They are ____________.

## C Listen and circle the correct pictures.

78

1. Q: What are they doing?

a  b  c 

2. Q: What are they doing?

a  b  c 

## D Listen and check the correct pictures.

79

Daily Test 6

# I Like to Run.

## A Listen, write, and match.

80

1. I can run.________ .

2. ________________ .

3. ________________ .

4. ________________ .

5. ________________ .

6. ________________ .

7. ________________ .

8. ________________ .

| run | fly | jump | swim |
|---|---|---|---|
| dance | sing | eat | cook |

## B Ask and answer the questions.

1.

A: Can you run?

B: Yes, ________. I can run fast.

2.

A: Can you fly?

B: No, ________. I can swim fast.

## C Listen and circle the correct pictures. 81

1. Q: Do you like to sing?

a 

b 

2. Q: Do you like to cook?

a 

b 

## D Listen and check the correct pictures. 82

Daily Test 7

# She Likes to Run.

## A Listen, write, and match.

83

1. He walks.
2. ______________
3. ______________
4. ______________
5. ______________
6. ______________
7. ______________
8. ______________

| runs | walks | swims | jumps |
|---|---|---|---|
| sings | dances | cooks | eats |

## B Ask and answer the questions.

1. A: What do you see?
   B: I see ________.
2. A: Does she like to sing?
   B: Yes, ________. She ____________.

**C** Listen and circle the correct pictures. 84

1. Q: Does she like to cook?

a 

b 

2. Q: Does it like to run?

a 

b 

**D** Listen and check the correct pictures. 85

1. 

2. 

3. 

4. 

Daily Test 8

# Where Did You Go?

## A Listen, write, and match.

86

1. go to a party
2. ____________
3. ____________
4. ____________
5. ____________
6. ____________
7. ____________
8. ____________

| go to school | go to the park | go to a movie | go to a party |
|---|---|---|---|
| eat cake | have a party | play with friends | watch TV |

## B Ask and answer the questions.

1. 

A: Where did you go yesterday?

B: I went to ____________.

2. 

A: What did you do?

B: I played ____________.

## C Listen and circle the correct pictures.

1. Q: Where did you go yesterday?

a 

b 

c 

2. Q: What did you do yesterday?

a 

b 

c 

## D Listen and number the correct pictures.

# Workbook Scripts

## Daily Test 1

### What Is It?

A
1. lion
2. tiger
3. elephant
4. giraffe
5. monkey
6. snake
7. zebra
8. hippo

C
1. A: What is it?
   B: It's a zebra.
2. A: What is it?
   B: It's a tiger.

D
1. Is it a giraffe?
2. Is it a snake?
3. Is it a hippo?

## Daily Test 2

### Who Are You?

A
1. girl
2. long hair
3. boy
4. short hair
5. cat 6. big eyes
7. dog
8. big ears

C
1. Do you have long hair?
2. Do you have short hair?
3. Do you have big eyes?

D
1. I'm a cat. I have big eyes.
2. I'm a dog. I have big ears.
3. I'm a boy. I have short hair.
4. I'm a girl. I have long hair.

## Daily Test 3

### Who's He?

A
1. my mother
2. my father
3. my sister
4. my brother
5. bird
6. rabbit

C
1. A: What does he have?
   B: He has a rabbit.
2. A: What does she have?
   B: She has a bird.

D
1. She's my mother. She has a rabbit.
2. He's my father. He has a bird.
3. He's my brother. He has a dog.
4. She's my sister. She has a cat.

## Daily Test 4

### What Are You Doing?

A
1. walking
2. running
3. eating
4. drinking
5. singing
6. dancing
7. cooking
8. washing

C
1. A: What is she doing?
   B: She's washing the dishes.
2. A: What is he doing?
   B: He's drinking water.

D
1. I'm a girl. I'm running.
2. I'm a boy. I'm singing.
3. She's my mother. She's cooking.
4. He's my brother. He's dancing.

## Daily Test 5

### What Are They Doing?

A
1. birds 2. flying
3. kangaroos 4. jumping
5. koalas 6. sleeping
7. dolphins 8. swimming

C
1. A: What are they doing?
   B: They are swimming.
2. A: What are they doing?
   B: They are flying.

D
1. They are kangaroos. They are jumping.
2. They are dolphins. They are swimming.
3. They are birds. They are flying.
4. They are koalas. They are sleeping.

## Daily Test 6

### I Like to Run.

A
1. I can run. 2. I can fly.
3. I can swim. 4. I can jump.
5. I can sing. 6. I can dance.
7. I can eat. 8. I can cook.

C
1. A: Do you like to sing?
   B: Yes, I do. I like to sing.
2. A: Do you like to cook?
   B: No, I don't. I like to eat.

D
1. What can you do?
   – I can run fast. I like to run.
2. What can you do?
   – I can swim fast. I like to swim.
3. What can you do?
   – I can jump high. I like to jump.
4. What can you do?
   – I can cook well. I like to cook.

## Daily Test 7

### She Likes to Run.

A
1. He walks. 2. She runs.
3. It jumps. 4. It swims.
5. He sings. 6. She dances.
7. He eats. 8. She cooks.

C
1. A: Does she like to cook?
   B: No, she doesn't. She likes to eat.
2. A: Does it like to run?
   B: Yes, it does. It likes to run.

D
1. What do you see?
   – I see a girl. She likes to cook.
2. What do you see?
   – I see a boy. He likes to swim.
3. What do you see?
   – I see a dog. It likes to eat.
4. What do you see?
   – I see a horse. It likes to jump.

## Daily Test 8

### Where Did You Go?

A
1. go to a party 2. go to a movie
3. go to the park 4. go to school
5. have a party 6. eat cake
7. play with friends 8. watch TV

C
1. A: Where did you go yesterday?
   B: I went to a movie.
2. A: What did you do yesterday?
   B: I watched TV.

D
1. I had a birthday party yesterday.
2. I ate cake.
3. I went to the park.
4. I played with my friends.

答案与译文

来，开始试试吗？

Unit 1
What Is It?
这个是什么？
A Let's Listen 听录音。
Listen to the Words. 听单词。
a. 听单词，说一说。
lion 狮子
giraffe 长颈鹿
monkey 猴子
zebra 斑马
b. 再听一遍，标出正确的图画。
Script 1. monkey 2. zebra 3. giraffe 4. lion
1.
2.
3.
4.
Unit 01 7

Listen to the Sentences. 听句子。
a. 听句子，说一说。
It's a lion.
那是狮子。
It's a giraffe.
那是长颈鹿。
It's a monkey.
那是猴子。
It's a zebra.
那是斑马。
b. 再听一遍，给图片标上正确的序号。
Script 1. It's a lion. 2. It's a monkey.
3. It's a giraffe. 4. It's a zebra.
3
2
1
4
8 Unit 01

Listen and Speak. 听录音，说一说。
使用下面的提问和回答进行练习。
What is it? 这是什么？
3 It's a monkey.
那是猴子。
2 It's a giraffe.
那是长颈鹿。
4 It's a zebra.
那是斑马。
1 It's a lion.
那是狮子。
Script
1. What is it? – It's a lion.
2. What is it? – It's a giraffe.
3. What is it? – It's a monkey.
4. What is it? – It's a zebra.
Unit 01 9

B Let's Listen More 再多听一些。

Listen to the Words. 听单词。 04

a. 听单词，说一说。

tiger 老虎 elephant 大象 hippo 河马 snake 蛇

b. 再听一遍，标出正确的图画。

Script 1. tiger 2. hippo 3. snake 4. elephant

10 Unit 01

Listen to the Sentences. 听句子。 05

a. 听句子，说一说。

It's a tiger.
那是（这是）老虎。

It's an elephant.
那是（这是）大象。

It's a hippo.
那是（这是）河马。

It's a snake.
那是（这是）蛇。

b. 再听一遍，给图片标上正确的序号。

Script 1. It's a hippo. 2. It's a snake.
3. It's a tiger. 4. It's an elephant.



Unit 01 11

Listen and Speak. 听录音，说一说。 06
使用下面的提问和回答进行练习。



Script
1. Is it a snake? – Yes, it is. It's a snake.
2. Is it a snake? – No, it isn't. It's an elephant.
3. Is it a hippo? – Yes, it is. It's a hippo.
4. Is it a hippo? – No, it isn't. It's a tiger.

12 Unit 01

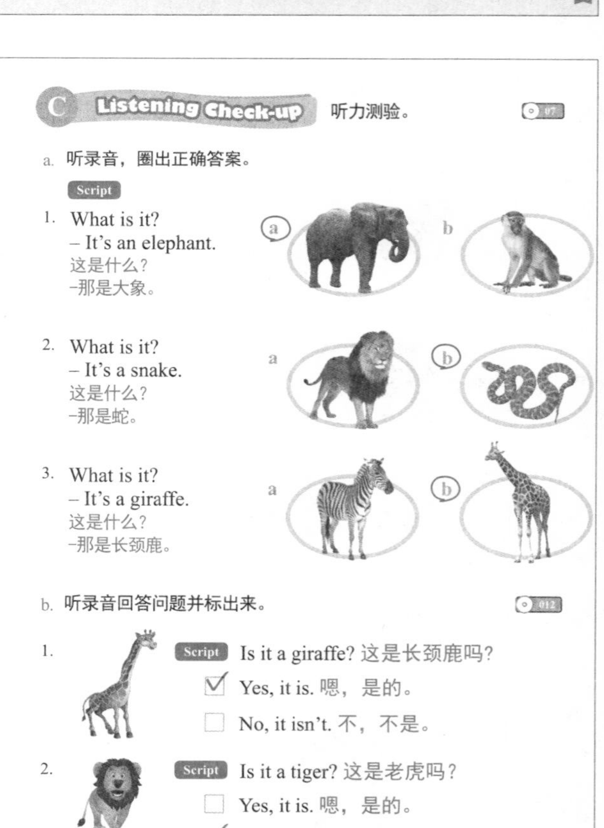

C Listening Check-up 听力测验。 07

a. 听录音，圈出正确答案。

Script

1. What is it?
– It's an elephant.
这是什么？
–那是大象。

2. What is it?
– It's a snake.
这是什么？
–那是蛇。

3. What is it?
– It's a giraffe.
这是什么？
–那是长颈鹿。

b. 听录音回答问题并标出来。 012

1. Script Is it a giraffe? 这是长颈鹿吗？
☑ Yes, it is. 嗯，是的。
☐ No, it isn't. 不，不是。

2. Script Is it a tiger? 这是老虎吗？
☐ Yes, it is. 嗯，是的。
☑ No, it isn't. 不，不是。

Unit 01 13

**D Let's Speak** 说一说。
使用下面的提问和回答进行练习。 08

What is it?
这是什么？

It's a tiger.
这是老虎。

**Your Turn** 轮到小朋友来问一问，答一答了。

**What is it?**
**– It's a giraffe.**
这是什么？
–这是长颈鹿。

**What is it?**
**– It's a monkey.**
这是什么？
–这是猴子。

**What is it?**
**– It's an elephant.**
这是什么？
–这是大象。

**What is it?**
**– It's a hippo.**
这是什么？
–这是河马。

**What is it?**
**– It's a zebra.**
这是什么？
–这是斑马。

14 Unit 01

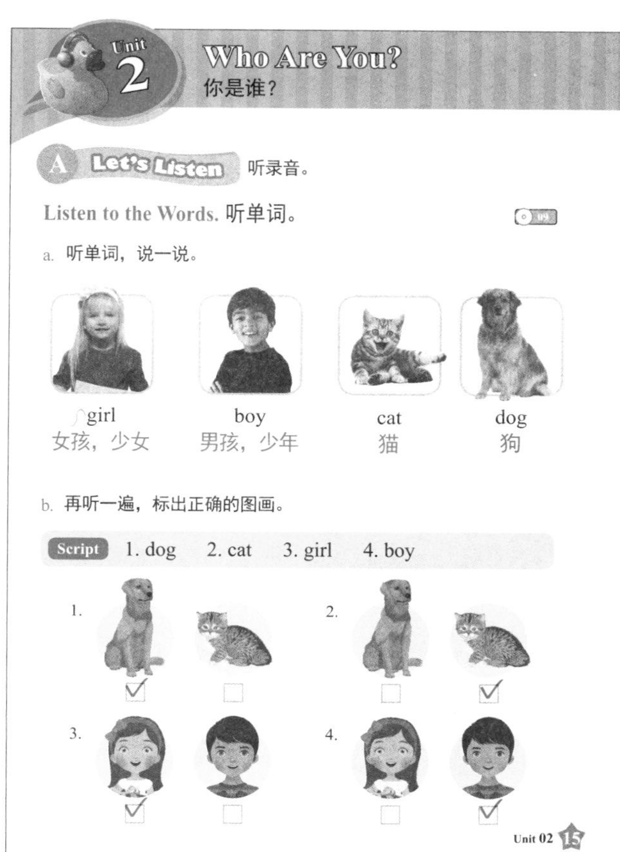

Unit 2 **Who Are You?**
你是谁？

**A Let's Listen** 听录音。

**Listen to the Words.** 听单词。 09

a. 听单词，说一说。

| girl | boy | cat | dog |
|---|---|---|---|
| 女孩，少女 | 男孩，少年 | 猫 | 狗 |

b. 再听一遍，标出正确的图画。

**Script** 1. dog 2. cat 3. girl 4. boy

1. ☑ ☐
2. ☐ ☑
3. ☑ ☐
4. ☐ ☑

Unit 02 15

**Listen to the Sentences.** 听句子。 10

a. 听句子，说一说。

I'm a girl.
我是女孩。

I'm a boy.
我是男孩。

I'm a cat.
我是只猫。

I'm a dog.
我是只狗。

b. 再听一遍，给图片标上正确的序号。

**Script** 1. I'm a boy. 2. I'm a girl.
3. I'm a dog. 4. I'm a cat.

1 3 4 2

16 Unit 02

**Listen and Speak.** 听录音，说一说。 11
使用下面的提问和回答进行练习。

Who are you? 你是谁？

② Hi. I'm **Tom**. 你好，我是汤姆。
I'm **a boy**. 我是男孩。

① Hi. I'm **Jane**. 你好，我是简。
I'm **a girl**. 我是女孩。

③ Hi. I'm **Lulu**. 你好，我是露露。
I'm **a cat**. 我是只猫。

④ Hi. I'm **Toto**. 你好，我是图图。
I'm **a dog**. 我是只狗。

**Script**
1. Who are you? – Hi. I'm Jane. I'm a girl.
2. Who are you? – Hi. I'm Tom. I'm a boy.
3. Who are you? – Hi. I'm Lulu. I'm a cat.
4. Who are you? – Hi. I'm Toto. I'm a dog.

Unit 02 17

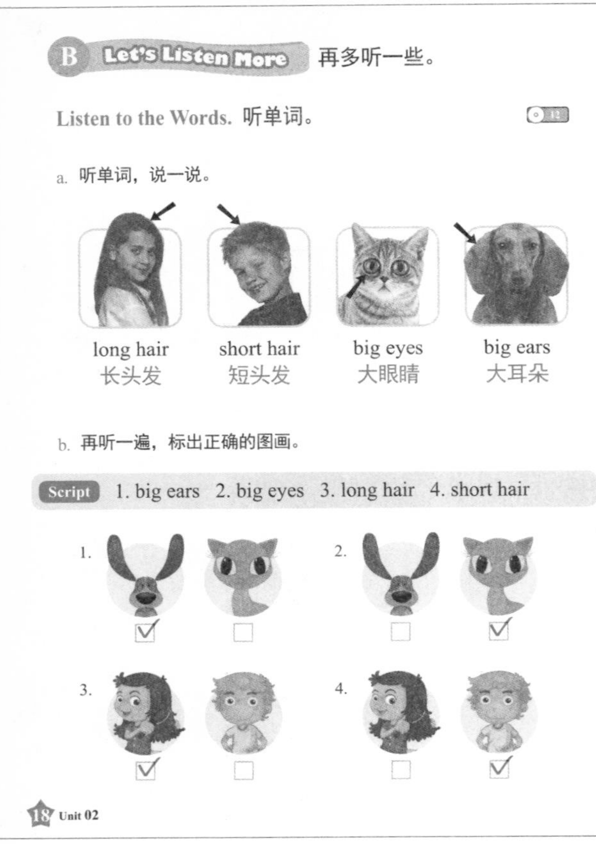

B Let's Listen More 再多听一些。
Listen to the Words. 听单词。
a. 听单词，说一说。
long hair 长头发
short hair 短头发
big eyes 大眼睛
big ears 大耳朵
b. 再听一遍，标出正确的图画。
Script 1. big ears 2. big eyes 3. long hair 4. short hair
18 Unit 02


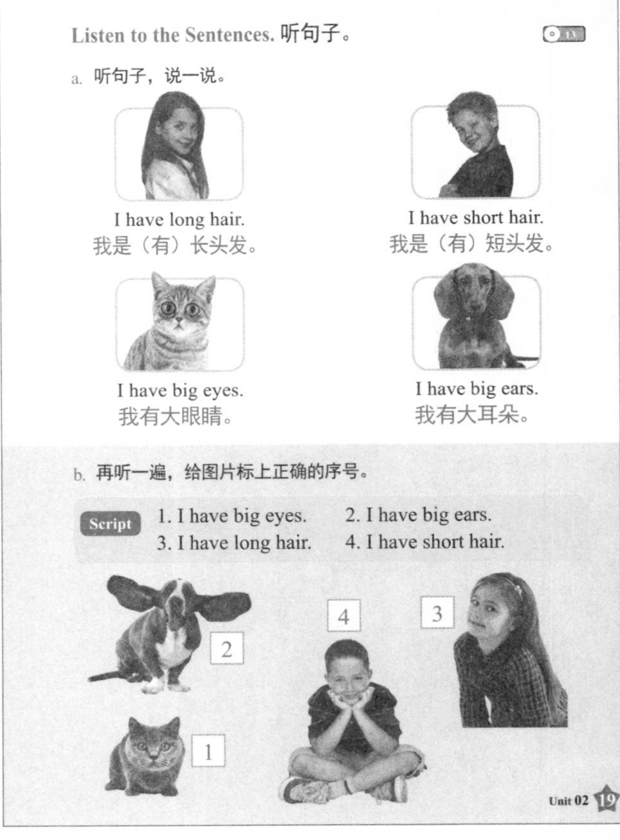

Listen to the Sentences. 听句子。
a. 听句子，说一说。
I have long hair.
我是（有）长头发。
I have short hair.
我是（有）短头发。
I have big eyes.
我有大眼睛。
I have big ears.
我有大耳朵。
b. 再听一遍，给图片标上正确的序号。
Script 1. I have big eyes. 2. I have big ears. 3. I have long hair. 4. I have short hair.
2
4
3
1
Unit 02 19

Listen and Speak. 听录音，说一说。
使用下面的提问和回答进行练习。
Do you have long hair?
你头发长吗？（你是长头发吗？）
1 Yes, I do.
I have long hair.
嗯，是的。
我头发长。
（我有长头发。）
2 No, I don't.
I have short hair.
不，不是。
我头发短。
（我是短头发。）
Do you have big eyes?
你眼睛大吗？（你有大眼睛吗？）
3 Yes, I do.
I have big eyes.
嗯，是的。
我的眼睛大。
（我有大眼睛。）
4 No, I don't.
I have big ears.
不，不是。
我耳朵大。
（我有大耳朵。）
Script 1. Do you have long hair? – Yes, I do. I have long hair.
2. Do you have long hair? – No, I don't. I have short hair.
3. Do you have big eyes? – Yes, I do. I have big eyes.
4. Do you have big eyes? – No, I don't. I have big ears.
20 Unit 02


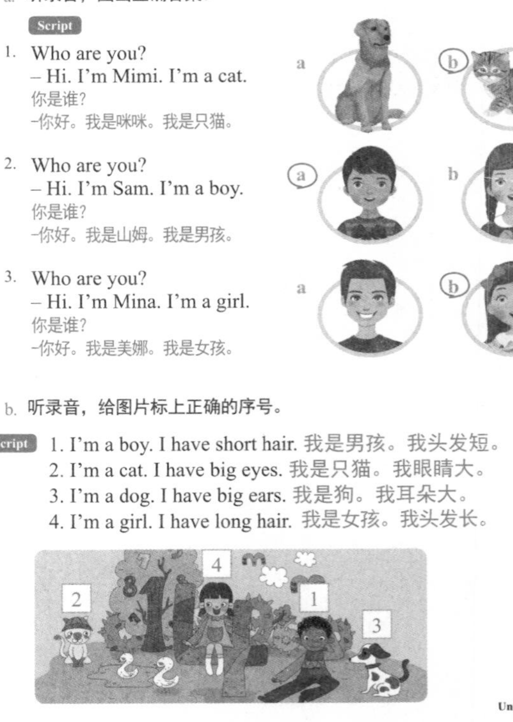

C Listening Check-up 听力测验。
a. 听录音，圈出正确答案。
Script
1. Who are you?
– Hi. I'm Mimi. I'm a cat.
你是谁？
-你好。我是咪咪。我是只猫。
2. Who are you?
– Hi. I'm Sam. I'm a boy.
你是谁？
-你好。我是山姆。我是男孩。
3. Who are you?
– Hi. I'm Mina. I'm a girl.
你是谁？
-你好。我是美娜。我是女孩。
b. 听录音，给图片标上正确的序号。
Script 1. I'm a boy. I have short hair. 我是男孩。我头发短。
2. I'm a cat. I have big eyes. 我是只猫。我眼睛大。
3. I'm a dog. I have big ears. 我是狗。我耳朵大。
4. I'm a girl. I have long hair. 我是女孩。我头发长。
Unit 02 21

D Let's Speak 说一说。
使用下面的提问和回答进行练习。
Hi. I'm Toto.
What's your name?
你好，我是图图。
你的名字是什么？
My name is Mimi.
我的名字是咪咪。
Your Turn 轮到小朋友来问一问，答一答了。
What's your name?
– My name is Minho.
你的名字是什么？
-我的名字是闵浩。
What's your name?
– My name is Mina.
你的名字是什么？
-我的名字是美娜。
Minho
Jinsoo
Mina
Ben
What's your name?
– My name is Ben.
你的名字是什么？
-我的名字是本。
What's your name?
– My name is Jinsoo.
你的名字是什么？
-我的名字是镇秀。
22 Unit 02


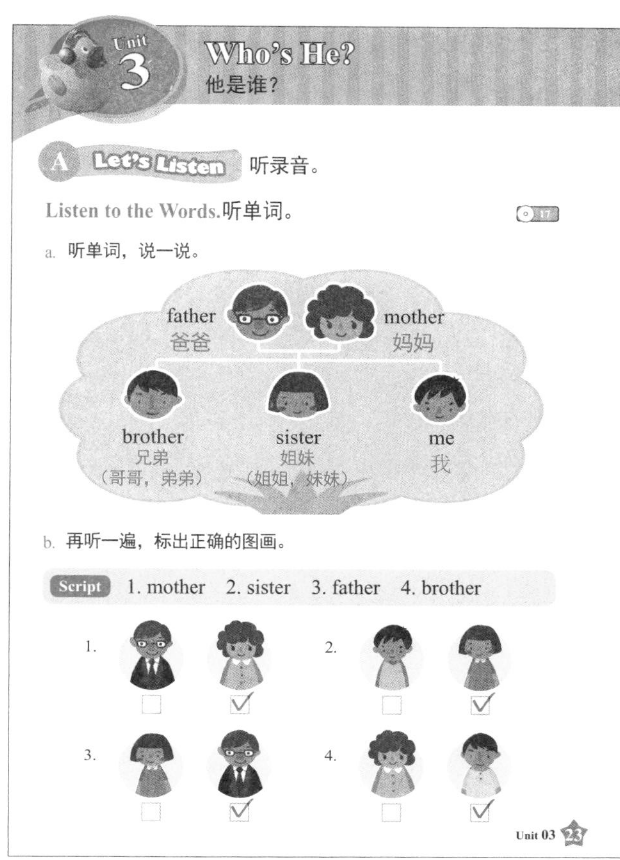

Unit 3
Who's He?
他是谁？
A Let's Listen 听录音。
Listen to the Words.听单词。
a. 听单词，说一说。
father
爸爸
mother
妈妈
brother
兄弟
（哥哥，弟弟）
sister
姐妹
（姐姐，妹妹）
me
我
b. 再听一遍，标出正确的图画。
Script 1. mother 2. sister 3. father 4. brother
1.
2.
3.
4.
Unit 03 23

Listen to the Sentences. 听句子。
a. 听句子，说一说。
He's my father.
他是我爸爸。
She's my mother.
她是我妈妈。
He's my brother.
他是我哥哥（哥哥，弟弟）。
She's my sister.
她是我姐姐（姐姐，妹妹）。
b. 再听一遍，给图片标上正确的序号。
Script 1. She's my mother. 2. She's my sister.
3. He's my father. 4. He's my brother.
1
2
3
4
24 Unit 03


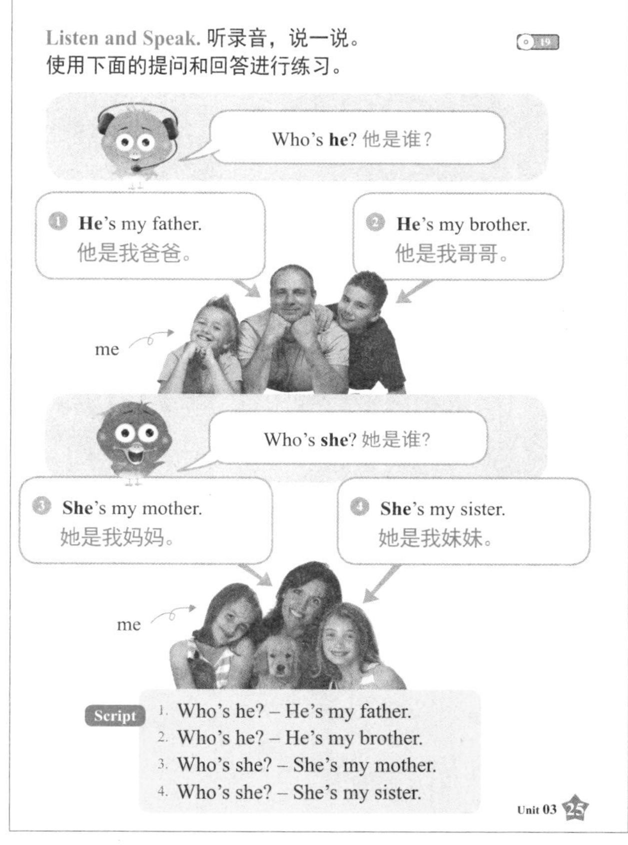

Listen and Speak. 听录音，说一说。
使用下面的提问和回答进行练习。
Who's he? 他是谁？
1 He's my father.
他是我爸爸。
2 He's my brother.
他是我哥哥。
me
Who's she? 她是谁？
3 She's my mother.
她是我妈妈。
4 She's my sister.
她是我妹妹。
me
Script 1. Who's he? – He's my father.
2. Who's he? – He's my brother.
3. Who's she? – She's my mother.
4. Who's she? – She's my sister.
Unit 03 25

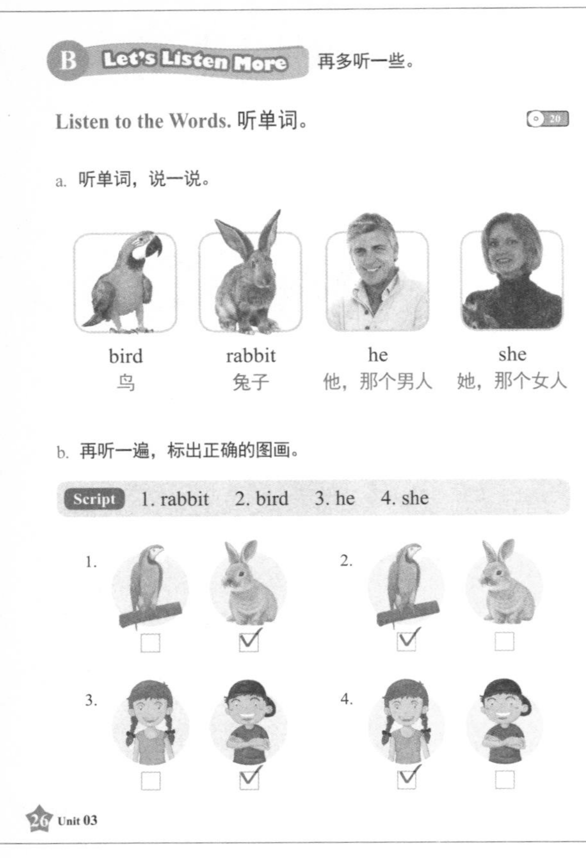

B Let's Listen More 再多听一些。
Listen to the Words. 听单词。
20
a. 听单词，说一说。
bird
鸟
rabbit
兔子
he
他，那个男人
she
她，那个女人
b. 再听一遍，标出正确的图画。
Script 1. rabbit 2. bird 3. he 4. she
1.
2.
3.
4.
26 Unit 03


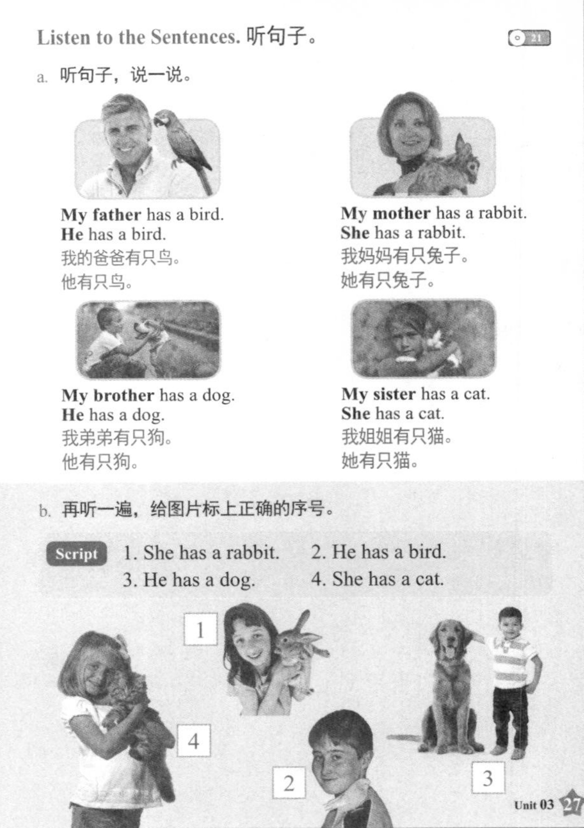

Listen to the Sentences. 听句子。
21
a. 听句子，说一说。
My father has a bird.
He has a bird.
我的爸爸有只鸟。
他有只鸟。
My mother has a rabbit.
She has a rabbit.
我妈妈有只兔子。
她有只兔子。
My brother has a dog.
He has a dog.
我弟弟有只狗。
他有只狗。
My sister has a cat.
She has a cat.
我姐姐有只猫。
她有只猫。
b. 再听一遍，给图片标上正确的序号。
Script 1. She has a rabbit. 2. He has a bird.
3. He has a dog. 4. She has a cat.
1
4
2
3
Unit 03 27


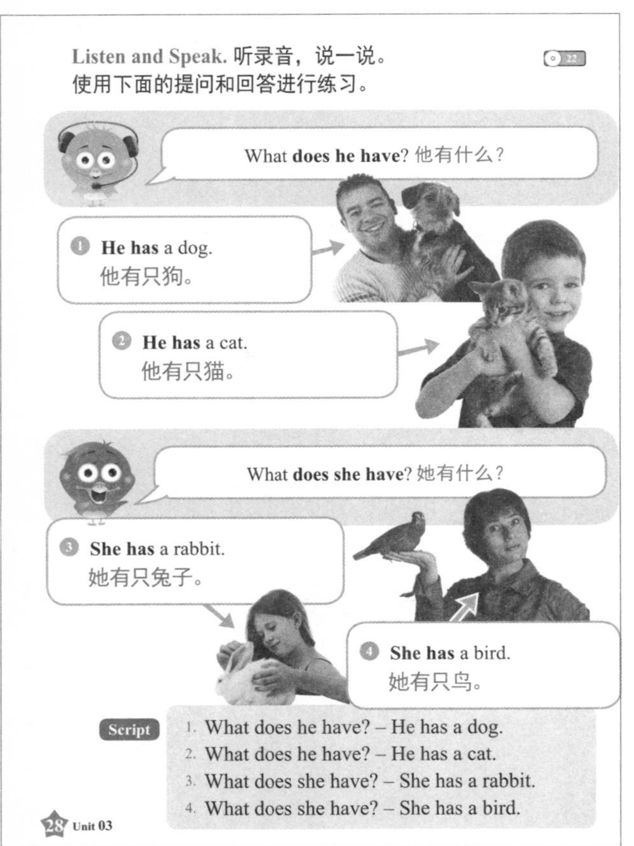

Listen and Speak. 听录音，说一说。
使用下面的提问和回答进行练习。
22
What does he have? 他有什么？
1 He has a dog.
他有只狗。
2 He has a cat.
他有只猫。
What does she have? 她有什么？
3 She has a rabbit.
她有只兔子。
4 She has a bird.
她有只鸟。
Script
1. What does he have? – He has a dog.
2. What does he have? – He has a cat.
3. What does she have? – She has a rabbit.
4. What does she have? – She has a bird.
28 Unit 03


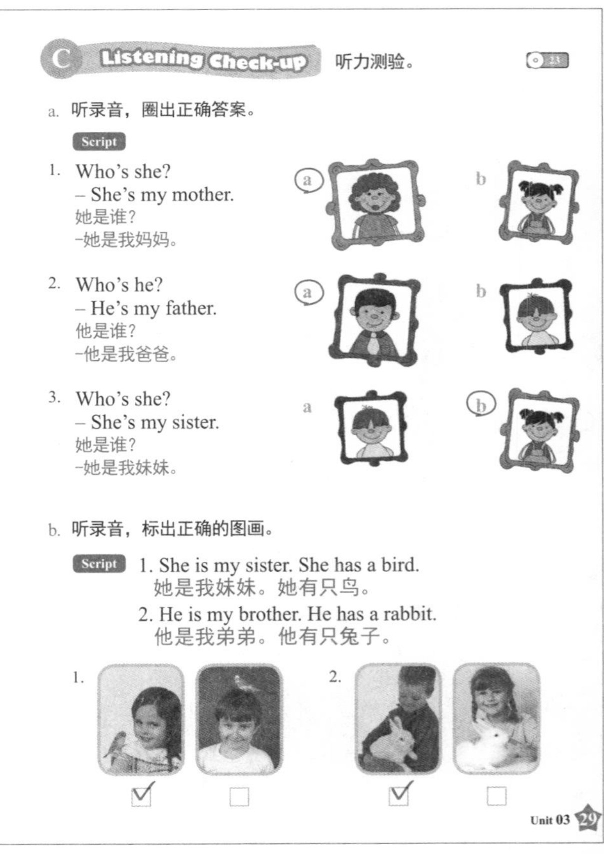

C Listening Check-up 听力测验。
23
a. 听录音，圈出正确答案。
Script
1. Who's she?
– She's my mother.
她是谁？
–她是我妈妈。
a
b
2. Who's he?
– He's my father.
他是谁？
–他是我爸爸。
a
b
3. Who's she?
– She's my sister.
她是谁？
–她是我妹妹。
a
b
b. 听录音，标出正确的图画。
Script 1. She is my sister. She has a bird.
她是我妹妹。她有只鸟。
2. He is my brother. He has a rabbit.
他是我弟弟。他有只兔子。
1.
2.
Unit 03 29

D. Let's Speak 说一说。
使用下面的提问和回答进行练习。

Who's he?
他是谁？

He's my brother.
他是我哥哥。

What does he have?
他有什么？

He has a dog.
他有只狗。

Your Turn 轮到小朋友来问一问，答一答了。

**Who's she?**
**She's my mother.**
她是谁？
她是我妈妈。

me

**Who's he?**
**He's my father.**
他是谁？
他是我爸爸。

**What does she have?**
**She has a cat.**
她有什么？
她有只猫。

**What does he have?**
**He has a bird.**
他有什么？
他有只鸟。

30 Unit 03

Unit 4 What Are You Doing?
你在干什么？

A Let's Listen 听录音。

Listen to the Words. 听单词。

a. 听单词，说一说。

| walking | running | singing | dancing |
|---|---|---|---|
| 走，正在走 | 跑，正在跑 | 唱歌，正在唱歌 | 跳舞，正在跳舞 |

b. 再听一遍，标出正确的图画。

Script 1. dancing 2. walking 3. running 4. singing

1. ✓ □　2. ✓ □
3. □ ✓　4. □ ✓

Unit 04 31

Listen to the Sentences. 听句子。

a. 听句子，说一说。

I'm walking.
我在走路。

I'm running.
我在跑步。

I'm singing.
我在唱歌。

I'm dancing.
我在跳舞。

b. 再听一遍，给图片标上正确的序号。

Script 1. I'm running　2. I'm walking.
3. I'm singing.　4. I'm dancing.

2　3　1　4

32 Unit 04

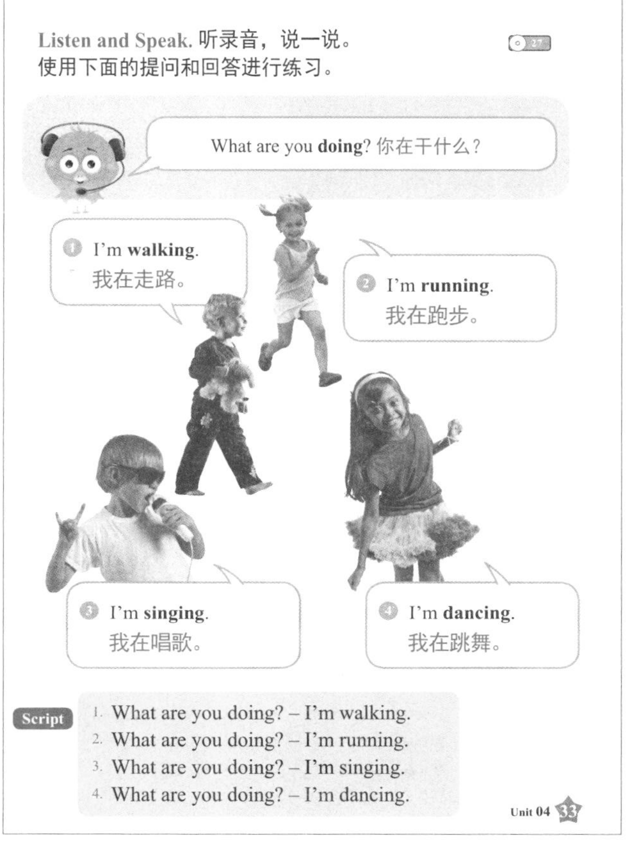

Listen and Speak. 听录音，说一说。
使用下面的提问和回答进行练习。

What are you **doing**? 你在干什么？

1 I'm **walking**.
我在走路。

2 I'm **running**.
我在跑步。

3 I'm **singing**.
我在唱歌。

4 I'm **dancing**.
我在跳舞。

Script
1. What are you doing? – I'm walking.
2. What are you doing? – I'm running.
3. What are you doing? – I'm singing.
4. What are you doing? – I'm dancing.

Unit 04 33

B Let's Listen More 再多听一些。
Listen to the Words. 听单词。
a. 听单词，说一说。
eating 吃，正在吃
drinking 喝，正在喝
cooking 做饭，正在做饭
washing 洗，正在洗
b. 再听一遍，标出正确的图画。
Script 1. drinking 2. cooking 3. eating 4. washing
34 Unit 04

Listen to the Sentences. 听句子。
a. 听句子，说一说。
He's eating pizza.
他正在吃比萨。
She's drinking milk.
她正在喝牛奶。
He's cooking.
他正在做饭。
She's washing the dishes.
她正在洗碗。
b. 再听一遍，给图片标上正确的序号。
Script 1. He's cooking. 2. She's drinking milk.
3. He's eating pizza. 4. She's washing the dishes.
1
2
3
4
Unit 04 35


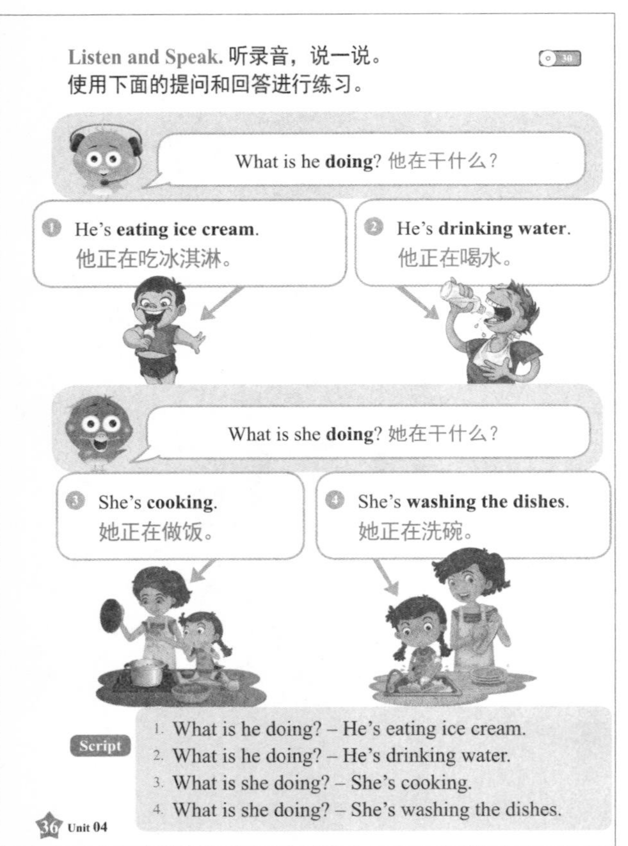

Listen and Speak. 听录音，说一说。
使用下面的提问和回答进行练习。
What is he doing? 他在干什么？
1 He's eating ice cream.
他正在吃冰淇淋。
2 He's drinking water.
他正在喝水。
What is she doing? 她在干什么？
3 She's cooking.
她正在做饭。
4 She's washing the dishes.
她正在洗碗。
Script
1. What is he doing? – He's eating ice cream.
2. What is he doing? – He's drinking water.
3. What is she doing? – She's cooking.
4. What is she doing? – She's washing the dishes.
36 Unit 04


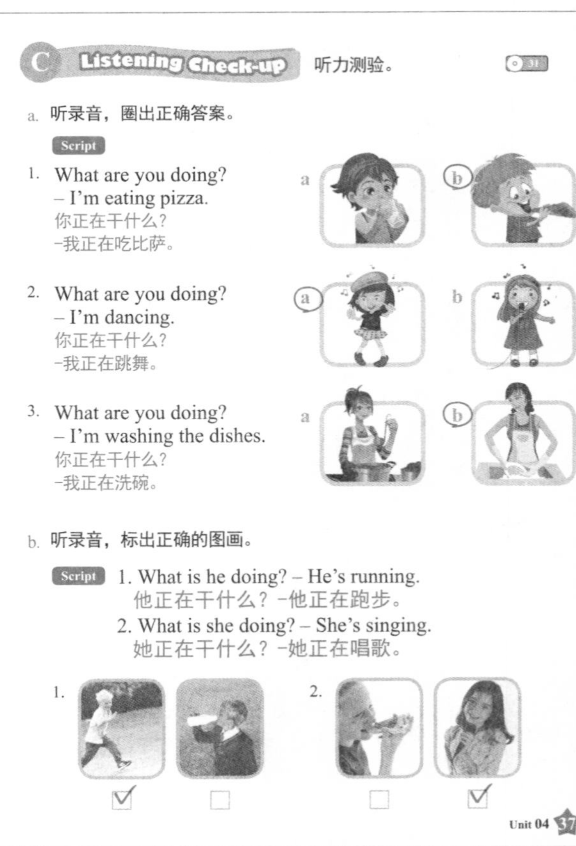

C Listening Check-up 听力测验。
a. 听录音，圈出正确答案。
Script
1. What are you doing?
– I'm eating pizza.
你正在干什么？
–我正在吃比萨。
2. What are you doing?
– I'm dancing.
你正在干什么？
–我正在跳舞。
3. What are you doing?
– I'm washing the dishes.
你正在干什么？
–我正在洗碗。
b. 听录音，标出正确的图画。
Script 1. What is he doing? – He's running.
他正在干什么？–他正在跑步。
2. What is she doing? – She's singing.
她正在干什么？–她正在唱歌。
Unit 04 37

D Let's Speak 说一说。
使用下面的提问和回答进行练习。 32

What are you **doing**?
你正在干什么？

I'm **walking**.
我正在走路。

Your Turn 轮到小朋友来问一问，答一答了。

**What are you doing?**
**– I'm dancing.**
你正在干什么？
–我正在跳舞。

**What are you doing?**
**– I'm singing.**
你正在干什么？
–我正在唱歌。

**What are you doing?**
**– I'm cooking.**
你正在干什么？
–我正在做饭。

**What are you doing?**
**– I'm drinking milk.**
你正在干什么？
–我正在喝牛奶。

38 Unit 04

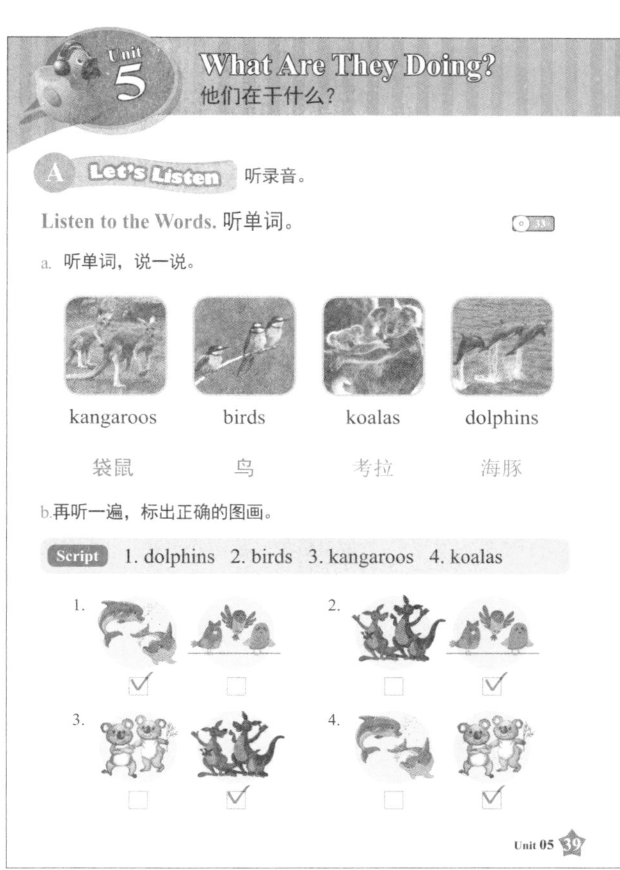

Unit 5 What Are They Doing?
他们在干什么？

A Let's Listen 听录音。

Listen to the Words. 听单词。 33

a. 听单词，说一说。

| kangaroos | birds | koalas | dolphins |
|---|---|---|---|
| 袋鼠 | 鸟 | 考拉 | 海豚 |

b.再听一遍，标出正确的图画。

Script 1. dolphins 2. birds 3. kangaroos 4. koalas

1. ☑ ☐
2. ☐ ☑
3. ☐ ☑
4. ☐ ☑

Unit 05 39

Listen to the Sentences. 听句子。 34

a. 听句子，说一说。

They are kangaroos.
它们是袋鼠。

They are birds.
它们是鸟。

They are koalas.
它们是考拉。

They are dolphins.
它们是海豚。

b. 再听一遍，给图片标上正确的序号。

Script 1. They are koalas. 2. They are kangaroos.
3. They are birds. 4. They are dolphins.

3 2 1 4

40 Unit 05

Listen and Speak. 听录音，说一说。 35
使用下面的提问和回答进行练习。

What are they? 他们是什么？

1 They are **kangaroos**.
它们是袋鼠。

2 They are **koalas**.
它们是考拉。

3 They are **birds**.
它们是鸟。

4 They are **dolphins**.
它们是海豚。

Script
1. What are they? – They are kangaroos.
2. What are they? – They are koalas.
3. What are they? – They are birds.
4. What are they? – They are dolphins.

Unit 05 41

B Let's Listen More 再多听一些。

Listen to the Words. 听单词。 36

a. 听单词，说一说。

| jumping | flying | sleeping | swimming |
| --- | --- | --- | --- |
| 跳，正在跳 | 飞，正在飞 | 睡觉，正在睡觉 | 游泳，正在游泳 |

b. 再听一遍，标出正确的图画。

Script 1. swimming 2. sleeping 3. flying 4. jumping

42 Unit 05

Listen to the Sentences. 听句子。 37

a. 听句子，说一说。

**The kangaroos** are jumping.
**They** are jumping.
袋鼠正在跳（跳高）。
它们正在跳。

**The birds** are flying.
**They** are flying.
鸟正在飞。
它们正在飞。

**The koalas** are sleeping.
**They** are sleeping.
考拉正在睡觉。
它们正在睡觉。

**The dolphins** are swimming.
**They** are swimming.
海豚正在游泳。
它们正在游泳。

b. 再听一遍，给图片标上正确的序号。

Script 1. The birds are flying. 2. The koalas are sleeping. 3. The kangaroos are jumping. 4. The dolphins are swimming.

3 1 2 4

Unit 05 43

Listen and Speak. 听录音，说一说。
使用下面的提问和回答进行练习。 38

What are they **doing**? 他们正在做什么？

1. They are **jumping**. 他们正在跳（跳高）。
2. They are **swimming**. 他们正在游泳。
3. They are **flying**. 他们正在飞。
4. They are **sleeping**. 他们正在睡觉。

Script
1. What are they doing? – They are jumping.
2. What are they doing? – They are swimming.
3. What are they doing? – They are flying.
4. What are they doing? – They are sleeping.

44 Unit 05

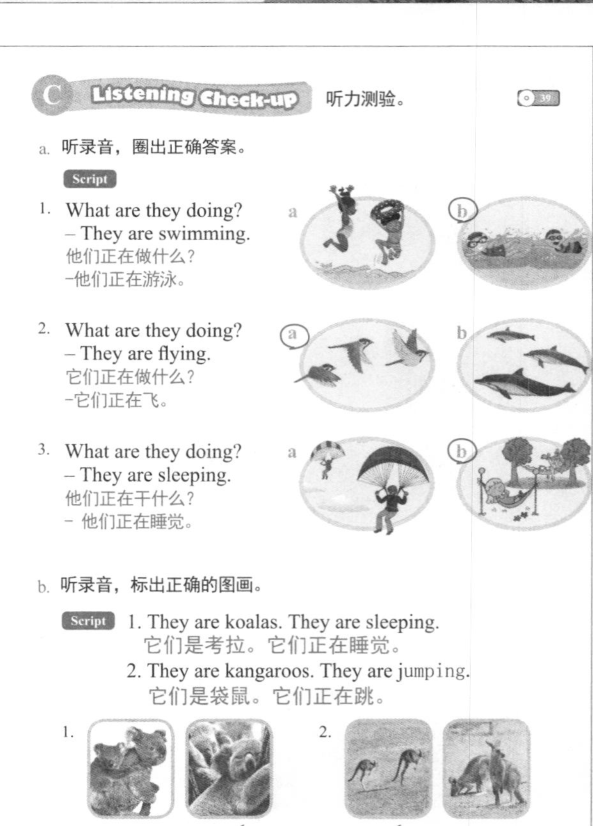
C Listening Check-up 听力测验。 39

a. 听录音，圈出正确答案。

Script

1. What are they doing?
– They are swimming.
他们正在做什么？
–他们正在游泳。
a (b)

2. What are they doing?
– They are flying.
它们正在做什么？
–它们正在飞。
(a) b

3. What are they doing?
– They are sleeping.
他们正在干什么？
– 他们正在睡觉。
a (b)

b. 听录音，标出正确的图画。

Script 1. They are koalas. They are sleeping.
它们是考拉。它们正在睡觉。
2. They are kangaroos. They are jumping.
它们是袋鼠。它们正在跳。

1. 2.

Unit 05 45

D Let's Speak 说一说。
使用下面的提问和回答进行练习。
What are they doing?
他们正在做什么？
They are running.
他们正在跑步。
Your Turn 轮到小朋友来问一问，答一答了。
What are they doing? – They are jumping.
他们正在做什么？
–他们正在跳。
What are they doing? – They are flying.
他们正在做什么？
–他们正在飞。
What are they doing? – They are sleeping.
他们正在做什么？
–他们正在睡觉。
What are they doing? – They are swimming.
他们正在做什么？
–他们正在游泳。
46 Unit 05

Unit 6 I Like to Run.
我喜欢跑步。
A Let's Listen 听录音。
Listen to the Words. 听单词。
a. 听单词，说一说。
run 跑
fly 飞
jump 跳
swim 游泳，潜水
b. 再听一遍，标出正确的图画。
Script 1. swim 2. fly 3. jump 4. run
Unit 06 47

Listen to the Sentences. 听句子。
a. 听句子，说一说。
I can run. 我能跑。
I can fly. 我能飞。
I can jump. 我能跳。
I can swim. 我能游泳。
b. 再听一遍，给图片标上正确的序号。
Script 1. I can swim. 2. I can run. 3. I can jump. 4. I can fly.
4
3
2
1
48 Unit 06

Listen and Speak. 听录音，说一说。
使用下面的提问和回答进行练习。
Can you run? 你能跑吗？
1 Yes, I can. 嗯，我能。
I can run fast. 我能跑得很快。
2 No, I can't. 不，我不能。
I can swim fast. 我能游得很快。
Can you fly? 你能飞吗？
3 Yes, I can. 嗯，我能。
I can fly high. 我能飞得很高。
4 No, I can't. 不，我不能。
I can jump high. 我能跳得很高。
Script
1. Can you run? – Yes, I can. I can run fast.
2. Can you run? – No, I can't. I can swim fast.
3. Can you fly? – Yes, I can. I can fly high.
4. Can you fly? – No, I can't. I can jump high.
Unit 06 49

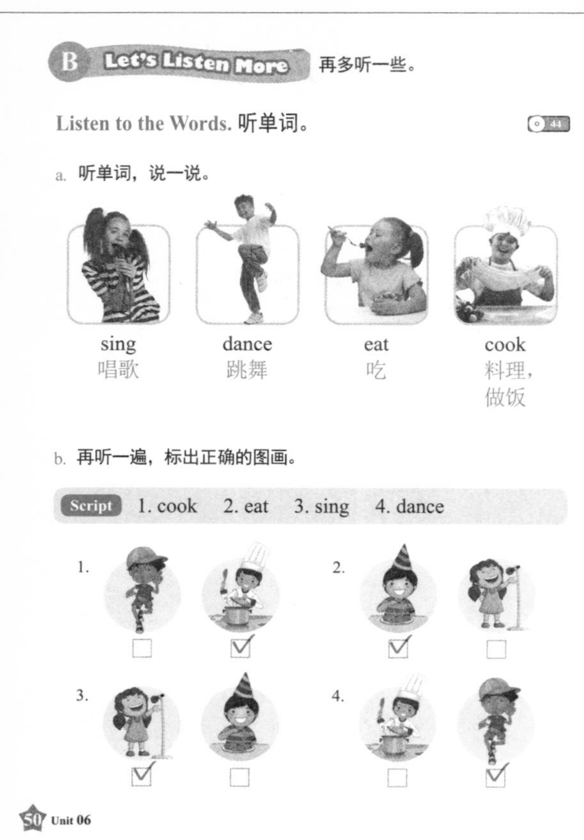

## B Let's Listen More 再多听一些。

Listen to the Words. 听单词。 44

a. 听单词，说一说。

sing 唱歌
dance 跳舞
eat 吃
cook 料理，做饭

b. 再听一遍，标出正确的图画。

Script 1. cook 2. eat 3. sing 4. dance

1. ☐ ☑
2. ☑ ☐
3. ☑ ☐
4. ☐ ☑

50 Unit 06

Listen to the Sentences. 听句子。 45

a. 听句子，说一说。

I **sing** well. 我擅长唱歌。
I **like to** sing. 我喜欢唱歌。

I **dance** well. 我擅长跳舞。
I **like to** dance. 我喜欢跳舞。

I **eat** well. 我很能吃。
I **like to** eat. 我喜欢吃东西

I **cook** well. 我擅长做饭。
I **like to** cook. 我喜欢做饭。

b. 再听一遍，给图片标上正确的序号。

Script 1. I like to sing. 2. I like to dance.
3. I like to cook. 4. I like to eat.



Unit 06 51

Listen and Speak. 听录音，说一说。
使用下面的提问和回答进行练习。 46

**Do you** like to sing? 你喜欢唱歌吗？
① **Yes, I do.** 嗯，我喜欢。
I like to sing. 我喜欢唱歌。
② **No, I don't.**
I like to dance.
不，我不喜欢。
我喜欢跳舞。
**Do you** like to cook? 你喜欢做饭吗？
③ **Yes, I do.**
I like to cook.
嗯，我喜欢。
我喜欢做饭。
④ **No, I don't.** 不，我不喜欢。
I like to eat. 我喜欢吃。



Script
1. Do you like to sing? – Yes, I do. I like to sing.
2. Do you like to sing? – No, I don't. I like to dance.
3. Do you like to cook? – Yes, I do. I like to cook.
4. Do you like to cook? – No, I don't. I like to eat.

52 Unit 06

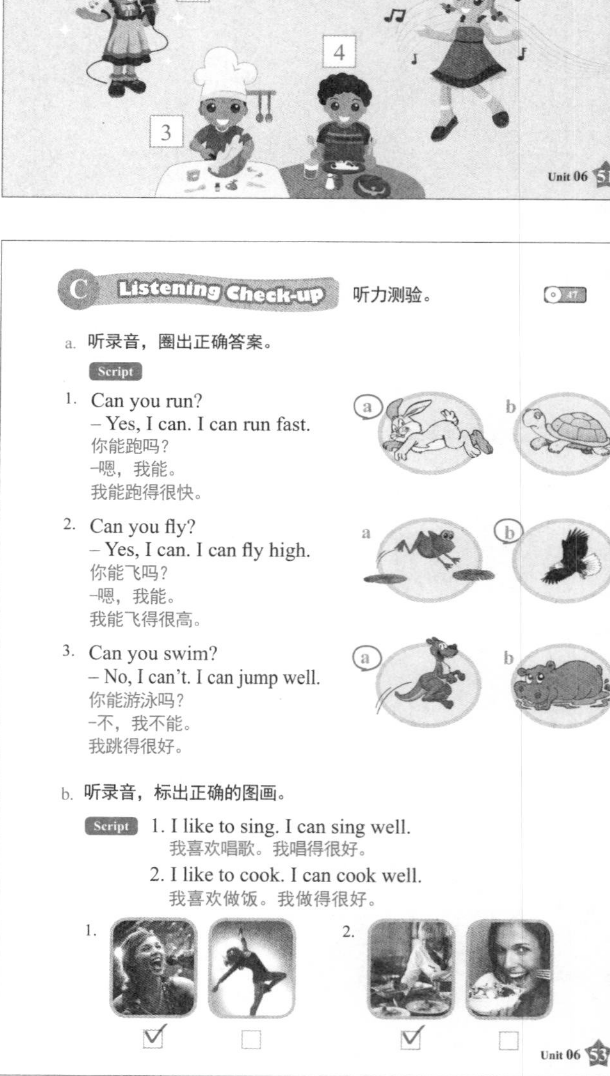

## C Listening Check-up 听力测验。 47

a. 听录音，圈出正确答案。

Script

1. Can you run?
– Yes, I can. I can run fast.
你能跑吗？
–嗯，我能。
我能跑得很快。
(a) b

2. Can you fly?
– Yes, I can. I can fly high.
你能飞吗？
–嗯，我能。
我能飞得很高。
a (b)

3. Can you swim?
– No, I can't. I can jump well.
你能游泳吗？
–不，我不能。
我跳得很好。
(a) b

b. 听录音，标出正确的图画。

Script 1. I like to sing. I can sing well.
我喜欢唱歌。我唱得很好。
2. I like to cook. I can cook well.
我喜欢做饭。我做得很好。

1. ☑ ☐
2. ☑ ☐

Unit 06 53

D Let's Speak 说一说。

使用下面的提问和回答进行练习。 48

What can you do?
你能干什么？

**I can** run fast. 我能跑得很快。
**I like to** run. 我喜欢跑。

Your Turn 轮到小朋友来问一问，答一答了。

**What can you do?**
**– I can swim fast.**
**I like to swim.**
你能干什么？
–我游泳很快。
我喜欢游泳。

**What can you do?**
**– I can jump high.**
**I like to jump.**
你能干什么？
–我能跳得很高。
我喜欢跳。

**What can you do?**
**– I can sing well.**
**I like to sing.**
你能干什么？
–我唱歌唱得很好。
我喜欢唱歌。

**What can you do?**
**– I can dance well.**
**I like to dance.**
你能干什么？
–我跳舞跳得很好。
我喜欢跳舞。

54 Unit 06

Unit 7 She Likes to Run.
她喜欢跑步。

A Let's Listen 听录音。

Listen to the Words. 听单词。 49

a. 听单词，说一说。

| walks | runs | jumps | swims |
| --- | --- | --- | --- |
| 走 | 跑步 | 跳 | 游泳，潜水 |
| 第三人称单数形式 | 第三人称单数形式 | 第三人称单数形式 | 第三人称单数形式 |

b. 再听一遍，标出正确的图画。

Script 1. runs 2. jumps 3. walks 4. swims

1. ☑ ☐ 2. ☑ ☐
3. ☑ ☐ 4. ☑ ☐

Unit 07 55

Listen to the Sentences. 听句子。 50

a. 听句子，说一说。

The boy **walks**. 男孩走路。
He **walks**. 他走路。

The girl **runs**. 女孩跑步。
She **runs**.她跑步。

The horse **jumps**. 马跳高。
It **jumps**. 它跳高。

The fish **swims**. 鱼游泳。
It **swims**. 它游泳。

b. 再听一遍，给图片标上正确的序号。

Script 1. He walks. 2. She runs.
3. It jumps. 4. It swims.

3 1 2 4

56 Unit 07

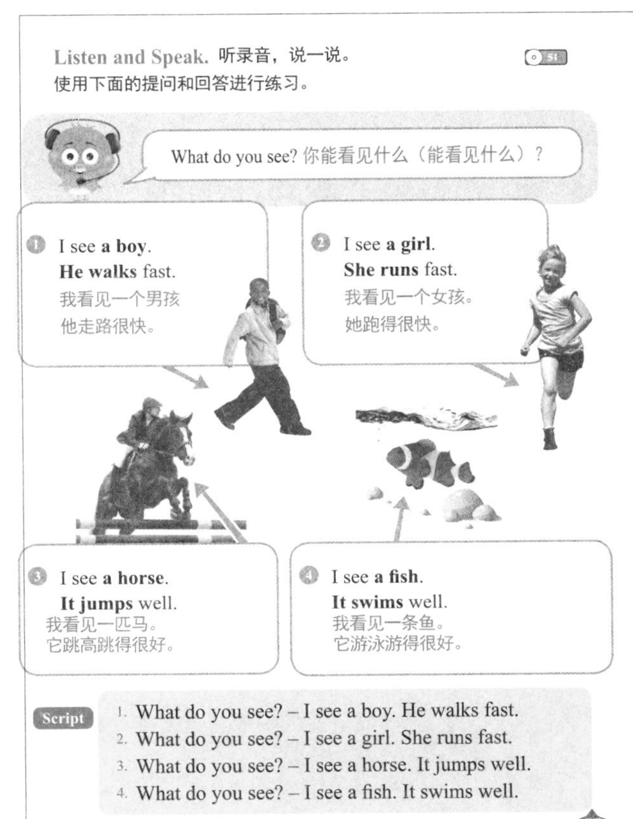

Listen and Speak. 听录音，说一说。 51

使用下面的提问和回答进行练习。

What do you see? 你能看见什么（能看见什么）？

1 I see **a boy**.
**He walks** fast.
我看见一个男孩
他走路很快。

2 I see **a girl**.
**She runs** fast.
我看见一个女孩。
她跑得很快。

3 I see **a horse**.
**It jumps** well.
我看见一匹马。
它跳高跳得很好。

4 I see **a fish**.
**It swims** well.
我看见一条鱼。
它游泳游得很好。

Script
1. What do you see? – I see a boy. He walks fast.
2. What do you see? – I see a girl. She runs fast.
3. What do you see? – I see a horse. It jumps well.
4. What do you see? – I see a fish. It swims well.

Unit 07 57

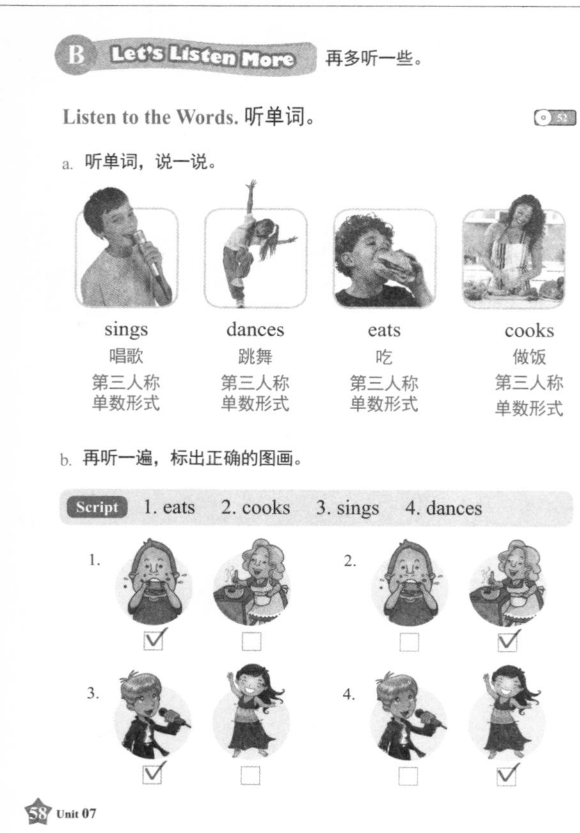

B Let's Listen More 再多听一些。

Listen to the Words. 听单词。 52

a. 听单词，说一说。

| sings | dances | eats | cooks |
| --- | --- | --- | --- |
| 唱歌 | 跳舞 | 吃 | 做饭 |
| 第三人称单数形式 | 第三人称单数形式 | 第三人称单数形式 | 第三人称单数形式 |

b. 再听一遍，标出正确的图画。

Script 1. eats 2. cooks 3. sings 4. dances

58 Unit 07

Listen to the Sentences. 听句子。 53

a. 听句子，说一说。

He **sings** well.
He **likes to** sing.
他擅长唱歌。
他喜欢唱歌。

She **dances** well.
She **likes to** dance.
她擅长跳舞。
她喜欢跳舞。

He **eats** well.
He **likes to** eat.
他很能吃。
他喜欢吃东西。

She **cooks** well.
She **likes to** cook.
她擅长做饭。
她喜欢做饭。

b. 再听一遍，给图片标上正确的序号。

Script 1. He likes to eat. 2. She likes to cook.
3. He likes to sing. 4. She likes to dance.



Unit 07 59

Listen and Speak. 听录音，说一说。 54
使用下面的提问和回答进行练习。

**Does he** like to sing? 他喜欢唱歌吗？

1 **Yes, he does.** 嗯，是的。
He likes to sing. 他喜欢唱歌。

2 **No, he doesn't.** 不，不是。
He likes to dance. 他喜欢跳舞。

**Does she** like to cook? 她喜欢做饭吗？

3 **Yes, she does.** 嗯，是的。
She likes to cook. 她喜欢做饭。

4 **No, she doesn't.** 不，不是。
She likes to eat. 她喜欢吃。

Script
1. Does he like to sing? – Yes, he does. He likes to sing.
2. Does he like to sing? – No, he doesn't. He likes to dance.
3. Does she like to cook? – Yes, she does. She likes to cook.
4. Does she like to cook? – No, she doesn't. She likes to eat.

60 Unit 07

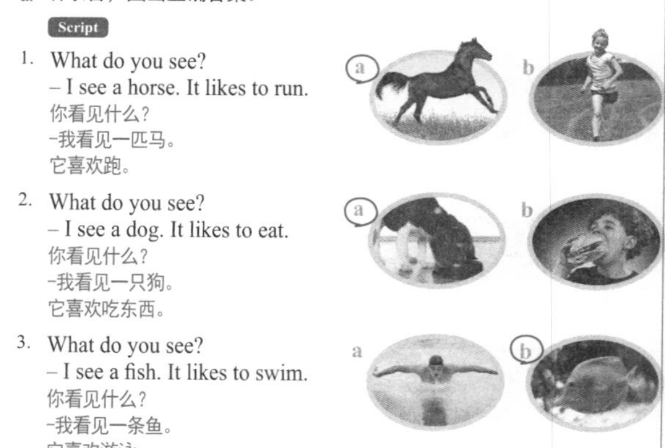

C Listening Check-up 听力测验。

a. 听录音，圈出正确答案。

Script

1. What do you see?
– I see a horse. It likes to run.
你看见什么？
–我看见一匹马。
它喜欢跑。

2. What do you see?
– I see a dog. It likes to eat.
你看见什么？
–我看见一只狗。
它喜欢吃东西。

3. What do you see?
– I see a fish. It likes to swim.
你看见什么？
–我看见一条鱼。
它喜欢游泳。



b. 能看出什么？听录音标出序号。

Script
1. I see a boy. He likes to walk. 我看见一个男孩。他喜欢走。
2. I see a girl. She likes to run. 我看见一个女孩。她喜欢跑。
3. I see a boy. He likes to cook. 我看见一个男孩。他喜欢做饭。
4. I see a girl. She likes to eat. 我看见一个女孩。她喜欢吃。

Unit 07 61

D Let's Speak
说一说。
使用下面的提问和回答进行练习。
What do you see?
你看见什么?
I see a girl.
She likes to dance.
我看见一个女孩。
她喜欢跳舞。
Your Turn 轮到小朋友来问一问，答一答了。
What do you see?
– I see a boy.
He likes to sing.
你看见什么?
-我看见一个男孩。
他喜欢唱歌。
What do you see?
– I see a girl.
She likes to eat.
你看见什么?
-我看见一个女孩。
她喜欢吃东西。
What do you see?
– I see a fish.
It likes to swim.
你看见什么?
-我看见一条鱼。
它喜欢游泳。
What do you see?
– I see a horse.
It likes to run.
你看见什么?
-我看见一匹马。
它喜欢跑步。
62 Unit 07

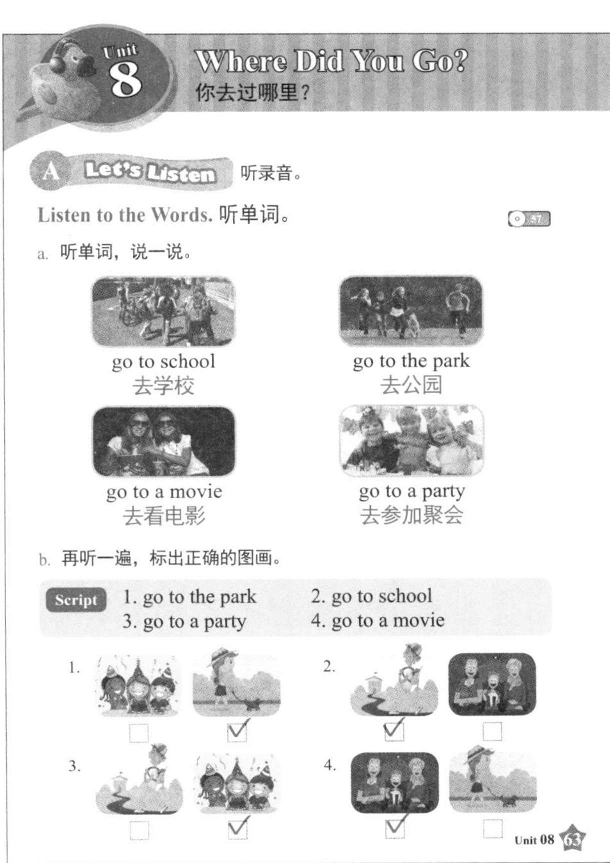
Unit 8
Where Did You Go?
你去过哪里?
A Let's Listen 听录音。
Listen to the Words. 听单词。
a. 听单词，说一说。
go to school
去学校
go to the park
去公园
go to a movie
去看电影
go to a party
去参加聚会
b. 再听一遍，标出正确的图画。
Script
1. go to the park
2. go to school
3. go to a party
4. go to a movie
Unit 08 63

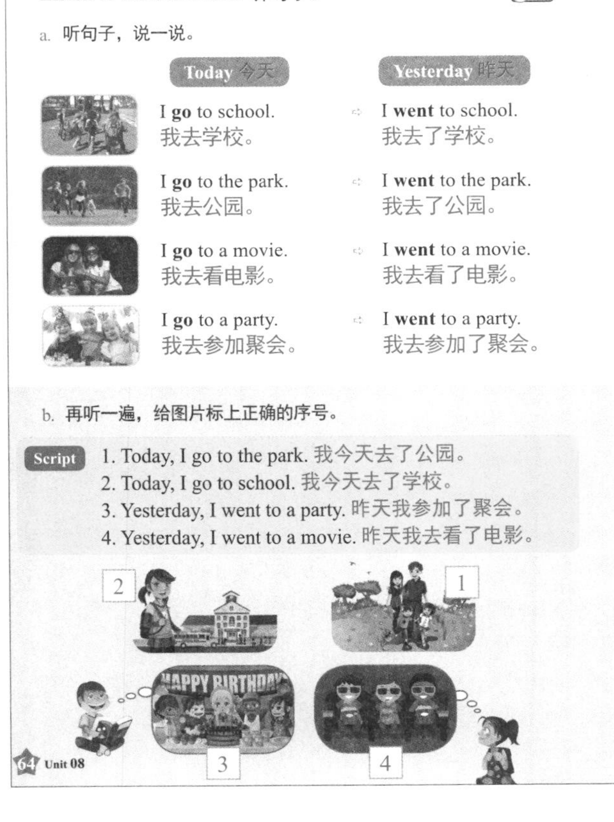
Listen to the Sentences. 听句子。
a. 听句子，说一说。
Today 今天
Yesterday 昨天
I go to school.
我去学校。
I went to school.
我去了学校。
I go to the park.
我去公园。
I went to the park.
我去了公园。
I go to a movie.
我去看电影。
I went to a movie.
我去看了电影。
I go to a party.
我去参加聚会。
I went to a party.
我去参加了聚会。
b. 再听一遍，给图片标上正确的序号。
Script
1. Today, I go to the park. 我今天去了公园。
2. Today, I go to school. 我今天去了学校。
3. Yesterday, I went to a party. 昨天我参加了聚会。
4. Yesterday, I went to a movie. 昨天我去看了电影。
2
1
HAPPY BIRTHDAY
3
4
64 Unit 08

Listen and Speak. 听录音，说一说。
使用下面的提问和回答进行练习。
Where did you go yesterday?
你昨天做什么了?
1 I went to school.
我去了学校。
2 I went to the park.
我去了公园。
3 I went to a party.
我去参加了聚会。
4 I went to a movie.
我去看了电影。
Script
1. Where did you go yesterday? – I went to school.
2. Where did you go yesterday? – I went to the park.
3. Where did you go yesterday? – I went to a party.
4. Where did you go yesterday? – I went to a movie.
Unit 08 65

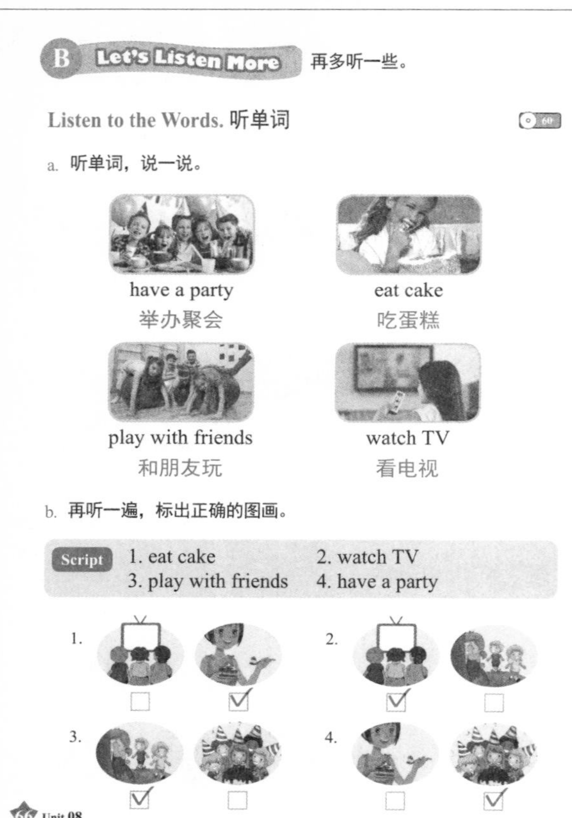

## B Let's Listen More 再多听一些。

Listen to the Words. 听单词

a. 听单词，说一说。

have a party
举办聚会

eat cake
吃蛋糕

play with friends
和朋友玩

watch TV
看电视

b. 再听一遍，标出正确的图画。

**Script** 1. eat cake 2. watch TV
3. play with friends 4. have a party

1. 2. 3. 4.

66 Unit 08

Listen to the Sentences. 听句子。

a. 听句子，说一说。

| Today 今天 | Yesterday 昨天 |
|---|---|
| I **have** a party.<br>我举办聚会。 | I **had** a party.<br>我举办了聚会。 |
| I **eat** cake.<br>我吃蛋糕。 | I **ate** cake.<br>我吃了蛋糕。 |
| I **play** with my friends.<br>我和朋友一起玩。 | I **played** with my friends.<br>我和朋友一起玩了。 |
| I **watch** TV.<br>我看电视。 | I **watched** TV.<br>我看了电视。 |

b. 再听一遍，给图片标上正确的序号。

**Script**
1. Today, I eat cake. 今天我吃蛋糕了。
2. Today, I play with my friends. 今天我和朋友玩了。
3. Yesterday, I watched TV. 昨天我看了电视。
4. Yesterday, I had a party. 昨天我开了聚会。

1 2 4 3

Unit 08 67

Listen and Speak. 听录音，说一说。
使用下面的提问和回答进行练习。

**What did you do** yesterday?
你昨天做了什么？

1. **I had** a birthday party.
我举办了生日聚会。

2. **I ate** cake.
我吃了蛋糕。

3. **I played** with my friends.
我和朋友一起玩来着。

4. **I watched** TV with my friends.
我和朋友一起看电视来着。

**Script**
1. What did you do yesterday? – I had a birthday party.
2. What did you do yesterday? – I ate cake.
3. What did you do yesterday? – I played with my friends.
4. What did you do yesterday? – I watched TV with my friends.

68 Unit 08

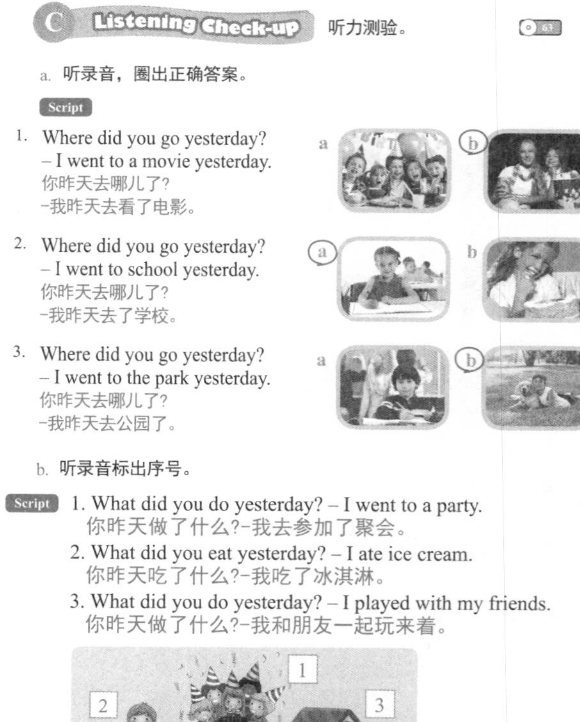

## C Listening Check-up 听力测验。

a. 听录音，圈出正确答案。

**Script**
1. Where did you go yesterday?
– I went to a movie yesterday.
你昨天去哪儿了？
–我昨天去看了电影。
a (b)

2. Where did you go yesterday?
– I went to school yesterday.
你昨天去哪儿了？
–我昨天去了学校。
(a) b

3. Where did you go yesterday?
– I went to the park yesterday.
你昨天去哪儿了？
–我昨天去公园了。
a (b)

b. 听录音标出序号。

**Script**
1. What did you do yesterday? – I went to a party.
你昨天做了什么？–我去参加了聚会。
2. What did you eat yesterday? – I ate ice cream.
你昨天吃了什么？–我吃了冰淇淋。
3. What did you do yesterday? – I played with my friends.
你昨天做了什么？–我和朋友一起玩来着。

1 2 3

Unit 08 69

D Let's Speak
说一说。
使用下面的提问和回答进行练习。
What did you do yesterday?
你昨天做了什么?
I went to school.
我去了学校。
Your Turn 轮到小朋友来问一问，答一答了。
What did you do yesterday?
– I had a birthday party.
你昨天做了什么?
–我举办了生日聚会。
What did you do yesterday?
– I ate cake.
你昨天做了什么?
–我吃了蛋糕。
What did you do yesterday?
– I went to the park.
你昨天做了什么?
–我去了公园。
What did you do yesterday?
– I played with my friends.
你昨天做了什么?
–我和朋友玩来着。
70 Unit 08